Ancient Rites of Odd Fellowship
Revisiting the Revised Ritual of the Order
of Patriotic Odd Fellows, 1797

LOUIE BLAKE SAILE SARMIENTO, J.D.

Text Copyright © 2020 Louie Blake Saile Sarmiento

Photo and illustration Copyright © are retained by original photographers, artists and owners except those that has since passed into public domain.

Editor: Cyril Jaymes N. Plantilla
Transcriber: Jeff Nicolo K. Palad
Layout and Cover Design: Louie Blake S. Sarmiento

All rights reserved. No part of this book may be reproduced, stored in a retrieval system, or transmitted in any form or by any means, electronic, mechanical, photocopying, recording, or otherwise, without written permission of the author and copyright owners of the photos and illustrations in this book. Illegal copying and selling of publications deprive authors, publishers and booksellers of income, without which there would be no investment in new publications. You can help by reporting copyright infringements and acts of piracy to the author and publisher.

The moral right of the author has been asserted. While every effort has been made to trace the owners of copyright material reproduced herein, the author would like to apologize for any omissions and will be pleased to incorporate missing acknowledgements in any further editions.

ISBN: 978-1-7338512-3-7
Published in the U.S.A.

Contents

Preface i

Origin and History 1

Opening and Initiation Service 11

White or Covenant Degree 27

Royal Blue Degree 35

Pink or Merit Degree 41

Royal Arch of Titus or Fidelity Degree 47

Merger and Succession 57

About the Author 61

Notes 63

References 65

Archive section at the International Headquarters of The Sovereign Grand Lodge of the Independent Order of Odd Fellows in Winston-Salem, North Carolina, U.S.A.

Preface

This book, *Ancient Rites of Odd Fellowship: Revisiting the Revised Ritual of the Order of Patriotic Odd Fellows, 1797*, is published for preservation and educational purposes. This is for the benefit of members, scholars, researchers and historians alike who want to gain more knowledge about the origins, history and evolution of the ancient rites of Odd Fellowship. It is not the objective of this book to divulge the secret workings of Odd Fellowship to the uninitiated. This ritual have been published to the public in the past and copies are available in public libraries. This is also considered ancient and no longer practiced by existing Odd Fellows' organizations today.

Odd Fellowship is one of the oldest fraternal societies in the world noting that the oldest documented lodge dates back on or before 1730. Recently, its obscure history and rites have been the subject of inquiry and discussion among members, researchers, scholars and historians alike. However, many complain that access to historical documents related to this ancient fraternity is very limited if not almost impossible. Admittedly, modern literature on the topic of Odd Fellowship is very scarce and the old records of this fraternal society are not well-preserved.

For how many years, a number of lodges almost secreted themselves to death to the point that majority of the younger generations today do not even know that this fraternity still exists. Many of its current members also fail to appreciate its history and a number have lost touch of its early traditions. A Past Sovereign Grand Master of the Independent Order of Odd Fellows once said that "*The true effort to revitalize Odd Fellowship should be to educate and inform its own members. Knowledge leads to confidence; confidence leads to enthusiasm; enthusiasm leads to commitment; commitment leads to pride; and these collectively leads to success.*" My advocacy is to help educate the current members and potential members about Odd Fellowship, its history, origins, traditions, teachings and significance. I can only do so little. That is to make information about this ancient fraternity easily accessible to younger generations in hope that they will eventually join and become dedicated Odd Fellows.

Origin and History

Fraternities and brotherhoods existed since the beginning of early civilizations - first among sworn kinsmen, monks, knights, Roman *collegia*, craft guilds, burial clubs, and later into fraternal orders and civic clubs. It is human nature that people desire to associate with each other either for social, philosophical, political, religious, charitable, mutual-benefit, or business purposes. The ancient mysteries, for example, played a vital part among the early Mediterranean civilizations. During the middle Ages, Orders of Knighthood, revolutionary brotherhoods and craft guilds existed and were part of the social order. During the industrial revolution, fraternal orders became numerous "to meet the social and economic needs of people whose very lives were affected by the shift from agrarianism to industrialism.[1] The Odd Fellows, as well as several other fraternal orders or friendly societies, appear to have evolved or inherited ideas from these numerous early sources.[2]

The mythical history of Odd Fellowship narrates that this Order was first established among the Jewish legion of the Roman Army during the reign of Nero about 55 A.D. Some twenty-four years later, Titus Caesar, observing the singularity of their notions and their camaraderie and their uncanny ability to recognize each other by signs even at night, called them Odd Fellows.

Guilds and Brotherhoods

The origin of fraternal orders can be more clearly traced from the demise of guilds in England and Scotland.[3] The historical connections are manifest in the rituals, terminology and functions shared by both the guilds and fraternal orders. In England and Scotland, organizations and clubs with benefit systems took the form of the guilds and reach back to the middle Ages. Even as far back as early in the 14th century, the early guilds were charitable associations, giving relief in sickness and adversity, and making provision for old age and for burial, and in this can be seen the origin of Odd Fellowship. Great good was done by these old English guilds, and in respect they are forerunners of fraternal orders which under the government of free and enlightened principles and on the soil of an English-speaking people, finally culminated into the Odd Fellows.

Contrary to popular misconception, it was not just the operative masons who guarded their trade secrets from others. Other craftsmen also joined forces and formed their own guilds or trade fraternities. In fact, there were more than one hundred early guilds in London alone during the middle Ages.[4] The *Fraternity of Butchers*, for example, owned a meeting Hall as early as year 975 and has charters dating back in 1605 and 1637. A record dating 1345 shows that the *Fraternity of Gardeners* petitioned the Lord Mayor to sell produce in front of the church of St. Austin. The Gardeners have charters dating back in 1605 and 1659 and a few other surviving documents in Scotland too. The *Worshipful Company of Carpenters* has charters dating 1477, 1558, 1560, 1607, and 1868 and controlled the craft with religious and charitable aims. There is a reference to the "Masters of the mysteries" of the *Fraternity of Cooks, Pastelers and Piebakers* from 1312 to 1438. These "Mysteries" suggest that they also have degrees of initiation and trade secrets.

A *guild* is a benevolent association of mutual-help that usually consisted of craftsmen belonging to the same trade or living in the same neighborhood.[5] They were sworn brotherhoods that had binding oaths to support one another in times of adversity and back one another in trade ventures alongside with their religious and ceremonial role. Meetings involved proper decorum and wearing of regalia such as chains of office, special robes and so on. They charged entrance fees and indulged in feasting and merry-making. They also had close ties with the church that many of the early guilds were often named

A Master Baker and his Apprentice.

after patron saints and their ceremonies usually had religious themes. Membership is ordinarily by apprenticeship which usually lasts up to seven years to learn the "mystery" of the trade. Upon completing apprenticeship, one becomes a freeman of his guild and may serve as journeyman, master, or set-up his own guild.[6]

Different types of guilds existed, including religious or social guilds, merchant guilds, and craft guilds.[7] Social guilds were termed simply as "guilds and brotherhoods" while the craft guilds were described as "mysteries and crafts". Within guilds are also offspring fraternities, clubs within clubs, exclusive for the elite of a particular craft including only the top men of the trade and other dignitaries.[8] Some guilds eventually admitted other people although they do not practice the same trade. The *Guild of Weavers*, for example, originally consisted of members of the trade when they were founded in 1155, but they later admitted sons of members and noblemen. The *Guild of Merchant Taylors*, on the other hand, admitted King Edward III as a member after they had lent him money to pay his wars. The *Company of Masons*' book of accounts mentioned a Lodge of "Accepted" masons in 1620 and 1621. This is the earliest reference to the Masons accepting people not practicing their craft. It was advantageous for guilds to admit noblemen because they increase the social prestige of their society.[9] The admittance of non-craftsmen eventually resulted into

While the Gardeners, Carpenters, and Masons were large enough to form their own separate guilds, a number of historians theorize that the Odd Fellows comprised a collection from all the other trades, which were not strong enough to form themselves to carry on a distinctive association.

the formation of two types of membership: *operative members* (those who practice the craft as a profession) and the *speculative members* (those who do not practice the craft but use the society as a vehicle for philosophical, social and charitable goals).

Similarly, Odd Fellowship presumably began as a guild or journeyman association in England. While major trades like the Masons, Gardeners, Carpenters, and Farmers were large enough to form their own separate guilds, smaller trades did not have enough numbers. As a result, people from smaller trades or those who exercised unusual, miscellaneous or odd trades joined forces to form their own trade association. These smaller groups were commonly known as *journeymen associations or companions* formed to defend their collective interests against the guild Masters and to provide food, lodging, and guidance for one another when they travel to search for work. As compared with the guilds, these associations usually consisted of Fellows and Apprentices representing numerous trades or crafts. They also have an elaborate initiation rite in which a young journeyman who joins the association will go through a system of degrees intended to test courage and loyalty and to ascend into hierarchy within the association. *The Prologue to The Canterbury*

Tales, written by Geoffrey Chaucer between 1387 to 1400, mentioned a company composed of journeymen belonging from different trades: "Well nine and twenty in a company of various sorts of people, by chance fallen in fellowship, and they were all pilgrims, who intended to ride toward Canterbury."

From Guilds into Livery Companies and Fraternal Lodges

When King Henry VIII broke-off from the Roman Catholic Church, he confiscated the properties of the guilds. Allegedly, he thought that they supported the Pope because of their link with the church. During the reign of Queen Elizabeth I, the *Statute of Apprentices* was passed which took the responsibility for apprenticeship away from the guilds.[10] The nature and scope of work was also changing, thus, the role of the guilds eventually went into decline. This removed an important form of social and financial support among ordinary workers. This allegedly resulted to a split between the operative and speculative Lodges. Operative guilds continued to survive as livery companies while speculative lodges adapted to the changing times and evolved into fraternal lodges and social clubs with a combination of social, moral and charitable or mutual-benefit functions.

During the mid-1600s to early-1700s, there seems to be a number of speculative lodges that were formed in England and Scotland. Some lodges of the speculative Masons allegedly evolved to become the *Free and Accepted Masons*. Some speculative Lodges of the Free Gardeners eventually formed into the *Order of Ancient Free Gardeners*. Several other fraternal lodges and clubs with a guild-like name, such as the *Order of Free Carpenters, Order of Free Fishermen, Order of Cabinet Makers*, and the *Order of Foresters,* also came into existence during the same period. What happened to the other guilds? One historian noted that the Odd Fellows is an "interesting deviation from the London Guild model."[11]

Early Benefit Clubs and Friendly Societies

Because record keeping was not held of much importance in the past and because most of the early records were destroyed as result of government regulations aimed at suppressing fraternal orders many years ago, it is admitted that the exact date of the first founding of Odd Fellowship is already lost in the fogs of antiquity. Admittedly, the first Odd Fellows had "originated in obscurity and was possibly not popular to claim any public attention of its early operations."[12]

There is strong evidence to suggest that Odd Fellowship is "an outgrowth of English Friendly Societies which were mutual associations formed for the payment of monetary benefits in times of incapacity for work due to sickness or injury, or death."[13] The first of these groups emerged in England as "a number of independent lodges or clubs comprised mostly of working-class people who were not rich, not royalty, and whose very lives depended on each other if ever one of their members got sick, became disabled, lost a job or died."[14] Like cooperatives and labor unions, they would contribute some of their hard-earned wages to a common fund which they could use for unfortunate times such as sickness, losing a job or death of a member.[15] By uniting themselves, they were able to build up funds to aid each other, their families and their communities in times of need. Such groups were known as *friendly societies or box clubs* and had been in existence since at least in the middle of the 17th century.

Daniel Defoe in his book, *Essay on Projects*, wrote about friendly societies in 1697 and defined them as "*a number of people entering into a mutual compact to help one another in case any disaster or distress fall upon them, and emphasized the contributory nature of these societies as a way to lower the poor rates and raise the self-respect of working people.*"[16] He recommended the creation of these societies as "a means to prevent the general misery and poverty of mankind and at once secure the country against beggars, parish poor, almshouses, and hospitals."[17] Other advocates shared the desire to use friendly societies to decrease the cost of poor relief. By the end of 18th century, a number of these clubs developed in virtually every English town and village.

Self-Institution

The early lodges followed the ancient usage of *self-institution*. This meant that any person can gather at least five people to form a Lodge without need of approval from any national association. These lodges differed from place to place. They had customs unique to themselves and these customs evolved from time to time. They had no Grand Lodge of any kind; they were all independent and separate lodges. Each lodge was presided by a Noble Grand Master and governed itself according to their own rules, traditions and practices. Hence, there were actually so many clubs or lodges named "Odd Fellows" but were not formally connected with each other.

They gave no benefits apart from helping widows and deceased members. The only one thing they had in common was a traveling assistance given to their members of various lodges who were traveling in search of work. If a member enters into an Odd Fellows Lodge in another town, he is given a traveling password and a certificate to show to the Lodge. He is then given assistance in terms of food and lodging. That money would then be reimbursed by one lodge to another. Unfortunately, they got into trouble between Lodges in reclaiming money so some lodges decided to form a Grand Lodge for better administration. The Order of Odd Fellows seems to be an amalgamation of these numerous small and independent lodges and clubs in England that eventually decided to unite themselves to form

George IV (1762-1830), while Prince of Wales, was admitted as a member of an Odd Fellows Lodge sometime in 1780.

a larger and more organized association. Fragmentary surviving records, newspaper accounts, and artifacts prove that the early Odd Fellows Lodges began to spread in England sometime in 1730 when various independent friendly societies or lodges united to form regional organizations or so-called "Unity."

Mergers, Acquisitions and splits

The first known *Affiliated Order* of Odd Fellows appear to be a result of amalgamation of these numerous self-instituted independent friendly societies and benefit clubs that eventually realized the need to federate themselves into a regional association for better coordination. Historical accounts demonstrate individual clubs that eventually organized themselves into a regional organization or later merged with existing *Affiliated Orders* and adopted the name *Odd Fellows*. Presumably, the first of the affiliated groups was the *Ancient Noble Order of Odd Fellows* which formed sometime on or before 1730. The Ancient Order had at least nine associated lodges by 1748. However, an *Improved Order of Odd Fellows* was successively formed as a schism from an earlier organization.[18] During the mid-1700s, some lodges in southern England further split and formed the *Order of Patriotic Odd Fellows*.[19] The existence of the *Patriotic Order* is proven by their Revised Rituals as approved by their Grand Lodge on March 12, 1797.

Within the lodges of the Order of Patriotic Odd Fellows, the term *"Grand"* was employed. This suggests that each Lodge was still sovereign and independent; hence, a *"Grand"* Lodge. The title *"Ancient Grand Master"* signifies that the person holding that position had "passed the chairs" as *"Vice Grand Master"* and *"Noble Grand Master,"* and whose office corresponded to that of the modern "Past Grand." The title *"Almoner"* is tantamount to that of the "Alms-distributor," and *"Recorder"* to that of "Recording Secretary." There was also a Warden who is stationed in the center in the order of business entitled "Harmony" (suggestive of social conviviality"; in the taking up of a collection for the sick and needy; regarding inquiries as to causes of absence at stated meetings; the colloquial system in conferring Degrees, etc.)

The rituals of the Patriotic Odd Fellows begin with the

By 1789, the Odd Fellows have already caught the attention of writers, caricaturists and artists in the United Kingdom. The early Odd Fellows started as an early form of social club in England with philosophical, social and charitable purposes. These groups held their meetings and initiations inside a pub or tavern. Although the meetings and initiations were formal and involved proper decorum, this is usually followed by a fellowship which included drinking, dinner, dancing, music and fun called the "harmony". The social side is held within the same meeting room because pubs and taverns in the past were not big enough to have a separate space for their festivities.

Opening and Initiation Ceremony. This is followed by four degrees, namely: Covenant; Royal Blue; Pink, or Merit; and Royal Arch of Titus, or Fidelity Degree. Each of the Degrees was conferred once every three or four months. Each degree usually ends with "Harmony" or social conviviality where food and beverages are served.

The rituals suggest that the Odd Fellows indeed originated from England especially noting the Judeo-Christian overtone. The oath or obligation in the degrees also required loyalty to the reigning monarch and the Constitution of England. But it should not be construed that Odd Fellowship is a Christian fraternity. The social context during the time when these rituals were revised should to be considered.

For a period of time, England was a highly Christian country ruled by a monarchy. When the French Revolution began in 1789, the English government became suspicious of large gatherings of ordinary people because of the possibility that these groups could be plotting against the monarchy. The English government responded by passing the *Rose Act of 1793* which required such societies to register given that they conform with the government's scrutiny of how they should be organized.[20] This was followed by the *Treasonable and Seditious Practices Act of 1795* which banned people from speaking or printing grievances or anything against the government and the *Seditious Meetings Act of 1795* which banned meetings of more than fifty people.[21] And when secret oaths, signs and passwords caught the attention of the authorities, the *Unlawful Oaths Act of 1797* was passed to illegalize oath-taking and various other methods in any society or association.[22] The latter law forced many fraternal orders and friendly societies to revise their rituals in 1797 to avoid being declared illegal and for its members to avoid arrest. Other fraternal orders even added the word "Loyal" to their organization's name to signify their loyalty to the English crown.

Opening and Initiation Service

(The Ancient Grand Master, Noble Grand Master, Vice Grand Master, Grand Secretary, Grand Treasurer, Grand Warden, and Grand Guardian, being robed, shall take their positions.)

N. G. M. - *(Standing in the East, taking the emblematical Sun in his right hand, shall strike twice. All the Grand Officers to stand up, with the exception of the A.G.M, who is to remain sitting, as if unconscious.)* Behold, the sun has arisen *(holding up the emblem)*. Grand Officers, it is time to commence our labors; Grand Secretary, call the roll of the Grand Lodge, *(On the name of the A.G.M. being called, he remains sitting and reclining, as if asleep.)*

N. G. M. - *(Looking toward the A.G.M.)* Our parent, from age and infirmity, still needs repose, Grand Officers, what is your wish? Shall I awake him, or proceed to our labor without him? The Grand Warden will ascertain your wishes.

(The G.W., having received a negative reply from all, is required to say:)

G.W. - Noble Grand Master, the Grand Officers are of opinion that our work cannot be commenced unless the full number are engaged therein, because we regard the teaching of mankind, so to live that they may know how to die, is similar to the act of creation, which we are taught was performed in seven days, and we should lack the counsel of the A.G.M. if any subject of difficulty should occur.

N. G. M. - That being the case, I will awake him. *(N.G.M leaves his place and touches the A.G.M., saying:)* Alas, my respected parent, the sun has arisen, and we are unable to commence our labors without your assistance. *(The N.G.M. resumes his seat.)*

A. G. M. - *(Standing with apparent difficulty)* My son, the days of man are of short duration, and it is our duty, with the help of God, to endeavor, even when the afflictions that attend advanced age press on us, to do our best for the good of mankind, although no longer able to bear the burden and heat of the day. Right glad I am that you did not attempt to work in an irregular manner. My weakness has now only been witnessed by the Grand Officers, whose knowledge of the heavy responsibilities of my office will be my excuse; but, if the eyes of our subordinates on their admission had been directed to my helpless condition, it would have been subversive of that discipline which conduces to order, which is Heaven's first law. My son, proceed to open this lodge.

N. G. M. - Vice Grand Master, where are you standing?

V. G. M. - (*With the emblem of the Moon*) In the West.

N. G. M. - Why in the West?

V. G. M. - Because I only rule in your absence, and as the sun goes down, apparently in the West, caused by the diurnal motion of the earth, although known to be a fixed body, in which course the moon also appears to travel, yet is an astronomical fact that her real motion is from West to East, in which direction I hope to move, with the consent, and approval of the Past Grand Officers.

N. G. M. - How do you hope to attain that position?

V. G. M. - By following your worthy example, and edifying, by the precepts you teach, I shall reflect the light borrowed from you, as the moon does that of the sun.

N. G. M. - Grand Secretary, where is your situation in the lodge?

G. S. (*With the Seven Stars in hand*) - In the North.

N. G. M. - Why in the North?

G. S. - Because the Pole star, that never changes its position in connection with our system, is there fixed.

N. G. M. - What do you deduce from that?

G. S. - My emblem is the Seven Stars, representing the constellation of Ursa Major, which contains the pointers of the Pole Star, and signified that the office I hold is to record with truth the proceedings of the lodge, that future generations may point with just pride to them.

N. G. M. - Grand Treasurer, what is your duty? And your position in this lodge?

G. T. (*With the crossed keys*) - In the North, also, To receive all

The Sun

The Moon and Seven Stars

The Heart and Hand

Opening and Initiation Service | **13**

fees, paid in accordance with the usages of this Order, and disburse the same under the instructions of the Grand Lodge.

N. G. M. - Grand Warden, where is your position in this Lodge?

G. W. *(With the Heart in hand)* - In the centre.

N. G. M. - Why in the centre?

G. W. - To preserve the harmony of the lodge which, like our Solar System, in which all the planets rotate around one common centre, I regulate and carry out the proceedings of our internal arrangements.

N. G. M. - Ancient Grand Master, where is the N. G. M. seated?

A. G. M. - In the East.

N. G. M. - Why in the East?

A. G.M. - Because in the East our ancestors perfected wisdom and the liberal arts of Geometry and Astronomy.

N. G. M. - What do you gather from this?

A. G. M. - That the N. G. M. is to us the representative emblem of Wisdom, which you have, according to the constitution of our Order, promised to disseminate for our benefit in the teachings of the lodge.

N. G. M. - Grand Guardian, where is your position in this lodge?

G. G. - Within the door of the Grand Lodge.

N. G. M. - Explain your duties.

G. G. - To see that no one is admitted without proper clothing, to receive the password of the degrees going forward, to receive the candidates in due form, after they are regularly prepared for initiation of our advancement, and to attend to the instructions of the Grand Lodge.

N. G. M. - Ancient Grand Master, what position is assigned to you in this lodge?

A. G. M. *(With the emblem of Mortality)* - In the Southeast, to the left of the N.G.M.

N. G. M. - What is your duty?

A. G. M. - To give that advice which my age and experience have qualified me to impart, to expound our constitution, to advice with the Grand Officers on all subjects of importance, and supplicate blessings on our proceedings.

N. G. M. - Our lodge being assembled with justice, perfection, and regularity. I request you to kneel and listen to the prayer of our A. G. M.

PRAYER

A. G. M. - Oh! Thou most Holy Creator of all things, and fountain of all good, bless our proceedings, and so influence the instructions of this lodge as to lead our brotherhood to adore Thee in spirit and truth. Amen.

N. G. M. - I declare this lodge opened for the instruction of brothers in the principles of true friendship and brotherly love.

N. G. M. - Grand Guardian, admit all who wait in the ante-room, in proper order.

(Subordinate officers, viz: Scene Supporters, Conductor, Almoner, and Recorder, to be admitted first; then brothers who hold no offices are to be admitted, singly. The Universal Sign to be given in front of the Grand Warden, who shall be held responsible for the correct giving of the same, or be fined according to the Constitution (rule 40).)

N. G. M. - Grand and Subordinate Officers and Brothers: Our lodge being now duly constituted, I shall proceed to business. Pay attention. If you have anything to bring before the lodge, be brief in your communications. Listen with attention to the words of instruction. Make no unseemly interruptions when a brother is speaking. In works of Charity, if need be, give according to your means. In conducting to the general harmony, be energetic and liberal. Remember our motto: *Tempus Fugit,* and therefore protract nothing unnecessarily. Fear God, and honor the King.

(The Grand Secretary will read the minutes of the last regular meeting of the lodge.)

N. G. M. - Officers and Brothers, you have heard the minutes of the last meeting. How say you? You that approve, stand up, you that dissent, be seated, while the Grand Warden makes up the number.

N. G. M. - Brothers, the business of the evening will be (*here name the business*) and to determine by lot upon the admission of Mr. _____, of _____ who was regularly proposed by Brother _____ , and seconded by Brother _____. I will thank the brothers appointed to report on the character of the candidate to state what they have ascertained, and I charge them to state the truth, the whole truth, and nothing but the truth, and that no mental reservation be made of either good or evil that has come to their knowledge.

(The report being made, and on the name being submitted to the lodge, if a majority be in favor, the Conductors shall go into the adjoining room to prepare the candidate thereto; the Almoner shall receive on signature the entrance fee of one point one shilling, together with the free-will offering of the intended brother. The Recorder and Almoner shall return to the lodge, when the Treasurer shall take charge of the fees, and the Grand Secretary shall take charge of the fees, and the Grand Secretary shall make a proper entry of the same in the Minute book.)

(The candidate is prepared for initiation by being divested of all his clothing, a hoodwink over his eyes, his arms pinioned by a cord, the ends of which are to be held by the Conductors. The keys are taken from the outer door to prevent either ingress or egress until the ceremonial of Initiation is completed. The Conductors each take one end of the cord and conduct the candidate to the door of the lodge, at which they give three knocks.)

G.G. - Who comes there?

Con. - Your Conductor, with Mr. _____, who has been well reported of, and since approved by the Brothers, has signed the petition and paid the regular fees, and now, as a son of Adam, comes to solicit from our N.G.M. instructions to guide him to discharge his duty toward his country and King.

(The G.G. reports the same, and orders to admit being given, the candidate is to be brought into the darkened lodge; strict silence to be maintained ; each brother present is masked. The Ancient Grand Master wearing a long white beard and wig, an apron of white leather bound in scarlet, with the emblems of mortality painted thereon, and on the pedestal before him, similar real ones. The N.G.M. to wear a yellow cloak, Vice G.M. a blue

cloak. The Treasurer, Secretary, and Almoner, in white surplices, to stand behind the altar of obligation. All the Grand Lodge Officers' aprons to be bound with purple, edged with gold lace.)

(The fittings for the initiation to consist of loose plants, to form the imaginary road, with rough knots left at intervals, some faggots of wood and bundles of cork, so arranged as to form rocks and forests, so constructed as easily to be removed, a small brazier with fire, a shower bath, and the usual theatrical appliances for the tempest scene.)

Initiatory Ceremony

(The candidate is brought before the Grand Warden, and reported by the Conductors, saying:)

Con. - We have, at this candidate's request, brought him here as a probationer, to be instructed in the proper duties of a Patriotic Odd Fellow.

G. W. - Stand where you are at your peril, presumptuous mortal! For thou little knowest what is about to befall you. Remember, the path that leads to happiness is not a smooth one. The road is long and rugged; new dangers meet you at every step. Are you willing to encounter all these trials in pursuit of knowledge?

Candidate - I am.

G. W. - That being the case, you will proceed at your own risk, but as I wish, as far as possible, to assist your researches, the Conductors who brought you hither shall accompany you, to prevent fatal injuries befalling you.

(The candidate, by the aid of the Conductors, moves on to the planks to make the round of the lodge three times.)

(The G.W., as the candidate walks, saying:)

G. W. - Remember, friend, other men, more worthy, perhaps, than yourself, have had to travel a similar path; therefore, be of good courage, for they only that endure to the end shall receive the reward.

(On the next circuit of the lodge, by an intentional jerk of the cord, the *candidate will lose his balance., and get among the cork; the Conductor, to keep up the illusion, saying:)*

Con. - He is gone over the rocks! Prevent him from falling into the quarry below, where so many have lost their lives.

(When fairly extricated, the G. W. says:)

G. W. - Friend, I feel for your condition, but right glad am I that you have passed this ordeal without personal injury, for many there are in life who rush into dangers, and having no guides, miserably perish. Think, when you return to the world and see the heedless and reckless plunging madly into dangers, what a benefit a friend or adviser would be to them; and, if possible, become that one yourself.

(The next round of the lodge, by a similar motion, the candidate is entangled among the brush-wood or straw, and a few gentle switches from green boughs complete the illusion. The Conductors saying:)

Cond. - We are in the forest and have lost the track.

(In the meantime, getting the candidate further entangled.)

Cond. - I see a light, and will make for it to gain information.

(In the meantime, the candidate is again cleared and the path resumed.)

G. W. - Friend, you have passed through another danger. This represents the dangers that flow from ignorance. How many of the human race perish as the victims of ignorance, , to whom, if right education had been afforded, the highest honors might have been awarded. When in the world, do all you can to counteract the evils that result from ignorance, and by your own example seek to educate all who come within your influence.

(The candidate is now brought near the brazier of fire, and by instantaneous contact is extorted an exclamation of pain, to which the G.W. says:)

G. W. - Many of the best of men have endured fiery trails in passing through the world; our records recounting the lives of the glorious army of martyrs who, being possessed of true knowledge, were enabled to sing praises to God in the midst of fire. Remember, when in the world, to aid and succor all who claim your protection when afflicted with trials and suffering, and thus commence a life of happiness, the result of peace of mind and good-will toward all mankind.

(The initiation concludes with the tempest scene. The gong sounds, chains rattle. Shot are rolled along the floor, sheets of copper are shaken, the brothers shriek or groan, while a deluge of water from a shower bath descends upon the candidate. On the signal, all is instantly silenced. The G.W. saying:)

G. W. - Friend, this scene represents the storms of life, when clouds and darkness are round about you, and dangers and difficulties thick strewn in your path, Learn from this scene to pity and sympathize with all unfortunates: when you hear of national calamities, remember the emblematical pains you endured.

(The candidate is now brought before the fire: the Conductors in the meantime removing as quietly as may be, the material used in the travel and tempest scenes:)

N.G.M. - Mr._____, you have passed through the emblematical scenes of danger, which I have no doubt will be remembered to your life's end, but there are other dangers that are real, and which will not even end with life, but will follow you into the unknown and invisible world. Are you prepared to make a promise to keep inviolate the proceedings of this lodge? Otherwise, we can proceed no further, and while in a state of darkness you will be removed beyond the lodge.

(The candidate having answered affirmatively, he is conducted to the altar, and, kneeling down, has one of his hands loosened, so as to lay his hand on the ten commandments, and repeated the following promise:)

I, _____, being in possession of my faculties, declare that I am free born, and of mature age, I follow no calling that oppresses my fellow man. I will never act as a bailiff, a bailiff's follower, or be a tipstaff or marshal man. I will act with justice to all men, I will be loyal to the King and Constitution, I will obey all laws passed by the High Courts of Parliament, I will pay all due respect to persons set in authority by the legal constituted rulers of this Kingdom. I will prefer a Patriotic Odd Fellow to any other in all my dealings, unles sI find reasons that justify me in acting otherwise. I will respect the virginity of his unmarried family, and the chastity of the married. I will never make known, either the whole or any prat thereof. All these covenants I promise and swear to obey, or suffer the penalty of having my arms

In 1797, the candidate is blind-folded, brought into the meeting room almost naked to symbolize birth, and assisted to walk on a set of loose wooden planks to symbolize the uncertainty of life. This rite was acceptable in the past but no longer performed since the beginning of the 19th century. However, the symbolic lessons have been preserved using other means.

and legs severed from my body, or be branded with infamy, such as my unworthy conduct would deserve.

    N.G.M. - The volume of the Sacred Law lays before you, and to render this obligation binding on your conscience, kiss the book once. *(Candidate kisses the book.)*

    N.G.M. - Give me your hand, that I may raise you as a newly initiated Patriotic Odd Fellow.

    Rise, a Brother Patriot. You have been bound and blinded to this time, but having, by solemn vows, bound yourself to act agreeably to our usages. I will restore you to the sense of seeing.

    (The pinions and bandage being removed, the lodge being still in darkness, except the light from the fire, the candidate is placed in front of the Gr. Warden, and is to be asked as fellows:)

    G. W. - Do you know anyone here? Look carefully to the East, West, North, and South.

(The Conductors to more the candidate in the directions indicated; but

on turning to the East, a transparency of a skeleton is visible, supported by two brothers. The Ancient G.M. sits by in a state of silence, until the Grand Warden calls his attention to an intruder being present. A.G.M arises, and resting one hand on a skull, raises one of the human bones aloft; saying:)

A.G.M -Who comes to disturb my meditations?

Candidate - Venerable Sire, I have heard the fame of your deep research in the hidden mysteries of science and knowledge, and I crave your instructions therein.

A.G.M - Mortal, how comest thou here without permission? For a heavy penalty awaits all who thus intrude themselves unbidden into my presence.

Candidate - Venerable Sire, I have traveled over rough paths, through deserts and mountainous districts, through dense forests, accompanied with storms of thunder and rain, caring for no external suffering, through my desire for knowledge.

A.G.M. - I am not satisfied with the whole of this statement, yet some portion bears the stamp of truth. My habitation is surrounded by a wall of fire, and none can approach without guides, who become answerable for such neophytes as they bring hither.

Candidate - Venerable Sire, I had some persons appointed to guide me in the path; otherwise the perils I have been exposed to must have proved fatal, and a voice followed me in my journey that encouraged me, after each trial, to still persevere.

A.G.M - That being the case, I will summon my court, who shall give judgment in this matter. Mortal, stand aside.

(The A.G.M. strikes the skull thrice, saying:)

A.G.M - There is an intruder who has gained access to my secret place of meditation, and by our usages all intruders must die, unless mercy be extended to them. I shall wait to hear somewhat in his favor. He has been asked if he knew anyone here; has had an opportunity to ascertain, but failed to recognize anyone.

Con. - A.G.M., I take the blame on myself, being the direct cause of bringing him hither. He has been spoken of favorably in the world, and our lodge, when properly constituted, agreed to his entering on the probationary trial. I have, with another trusty brother, attended his footsteps, and aided his own good intentions. He has passed through perils of no mean order, and having thus satisfied the lodge of his integrity, our N.G.M has administered the obligation to him, and raised him as a patriotic Odd Fellow.

A.G.M - I have heard this report which, joined to the plain statement made by the candidate, is something in his favor. Past and Present Grand Lodge Officers, what do you desire? *Ans.:* Show mercy. Subordinate Officers, what do you desire? *Ans.:* Show mercy. Brothers, what do you desire? *Ans.:* Show mercy.

A.G.M. - Stand on thy feet, mortal. The desire that has been expressed by the lodge is for mercy to be extended to you; but know that the power of life and death is still in my hands, representatively; yet as we all have need of mercy from the Great Ruler of the Universe, I will concede to the wish expressed in your favor. My son, give me your right hand, and I will endeavor to teach you to know yourself. Behold this emblem of mortality. It is the final close of life's eventful history. Its contemplation should daily solemnize your mind to prepare for another state of being, whenever the Wise Disposer of all events sees fit to summon you away. Where is the tongue from which flowed the eloquence that rendered its possessor the welcome guest of a hundred households? It is now silent, and cannot reply. The lips that were oft pressed to the cheeks of the loved ones, have ceased to reciprocate. The cheek that was looked on with fondness, and once bloomed with the promise of years, is now withered in the blast. The eye, with its lustre, is decayed and fallen from its socket. The aspiring thought, the imagination of the heart, and the whole of the intellect, that influenced society, are laid low by mortality, who, sooner or later, levels all in the dust. Mortal, this lot is thine! The king and the slave all share the same fate. Wealth, pomp or grandeur, are but the vision of today; tomorrow, eternity opens before them, and the stern king of terrors strikes them down, and with it the schemes of ambition, oppression, and aggrandizement, are brought to the naught. What though you now possess the strong arm, and the crimson cheek of glowing health, or the brain full of intellect? All become as nothing before the touch of the destroyer. Let the men whose ruling passions are either the accumulation of wealth, or obtaining place and position in the world, stand here and contemplate what they must come to, for it is appointed unto all men once to die. My son, seek to know thyself; realize the idea that your present life is only a probationary one, previous to entering upon an existence of eternal duration. Through life endeavor to check unruly passions; bear up nobly against adversity; do all the good you can to your fellowmen; correct yourself by the standard of truth, and having attained to this, you can wait calmly for Heaven's decree, and welcome the state of immortality, where the wicked cease to trouble, and the weary are at rest.

(The candidate here is required to bow in reverence, with his eyes closed, and in the meantime, the death scene is removed, and the lodge is relighted. The brothers are unmasked, and all are to assume a placid appearance.)

N.G.M. - Brother_____, you are doubtless surprised at the ceremonial you have undergone, and as you have been kept in personal discomfort for sometime, I will, as soon as I have explained the reason, order their restoration; but, before I do so, I request the Grand Warden to protect your secrets from the rude gaze of the brotherhood.

(The Grand Warden approaches with a plain, unadorned lamb-skin apron, ties it on with proper decorum, saying:)

G.W. - I now clothe you with the lodge badge of lost innocence, but it also has its antidote, for while the loss of innocence by the disobedience of our first parents disclosed to them that they were naked, and induced them to seek a covering for their shame; yet, the great atonement made for all sin, by the Son of God, was prefigured in the Mosaic Law by the sacrifice of animals, and of the skin of the sin offering you recovering is made.

G.W. - Noble Grand Master, your orders are executed.

N.G.M - Brother _____, your initiation is to be considered emblematical of the life of man. The lodge room is the world, and the death scene the end of life. "Naked you came in the world, and naked shall you go out of it," says Holy Writ. Then you were divested of all your clothing before coming into the lodge room, emblematical of your birth. The imaginary road was thick set with dangers. This is intended to represent the various straits and difficulties that man encounters in passing through the world, which is the probationary state, whence man is either confirmed in evil, as his passions, if uncontrolled, lead him captive, and thus, while on earth, he becomes fitted to dwell in company with demons, or else, regenerated by a belief in the word of God, and becomes fitted for a divine inheritance in the regions of eternal bliss. The hoodwink was placed over your eyes to denote that in our walk through life we are in darkness with regard to what shall happen to us on the morrow. The two cords represent the good or evil principles that actuate our motives, and thus preserve us in a general state of equilibrium. The death scene is intended as an emblem of your death to former principles, and that henceforth you begin a new life of usefulness, keeping the great end of living in view, viz: the perfect knowledge of yourself. You will now retire and assume your clothing, and return as soon as possible, to complete the lesson of instruction.

N.G.M. - Worthy G.W., instruct the G. Guardian to admit any who are waiting, when the candidate has resumed his clothing.

(The N.G.M. is now to transact the business of the lodge, by inquiries after the health or causes of absence of any brother reported as being absent. He orders relief in cases of distress reported on by the Almoner, and then proceeds to harmony, in accordance with the constitution.)

G.G. - The alarm is sounded.

G.W. - N.G.M., the alarm is sounded.

N.G.M. - See to the cause, and admit properly clothed brothers.

(When all are seated, and the candidate returned, to proceed thus:)

N.G.M. - Brother _____, the Conductors will lead you to your proper place to receive further instructions.

(The Conductors place the candidate in a chair, between the altar of obligation and the G.W.)

N.G.M. - Bro. _____, I have little more to say on this occasion, except to direct your attention to the glorious works of nature. If we take an attentive survey of the wonderful works of creation, and examine closely the objects that surround us, and rightly consider their nature and properties, our deepest admiration must be excited by studying the good order and proportions that govern the whole. The mind, capable of reflection, must irresistibly be drawn to adore the Almighty Being, who directs their operations. The science of astronomy lifts our minds above the world and its doings, and leads us to exclaim: "An undevout astronomer is mad." The sun, the centre of our system, diffusing light and heat to the world. The planetary system, of which our earth is one of the smallest. The starry skies, composed of thousands of suns, the possible centres of other systems. While, ever and anon, those magnificent displays of mysterious import, which we call comets, fly through unlimited space, for what purposes we know not, rendering man insignificant in comparison therewith. Yet, the word of God declares: "Man was created for His glory." Day and night fail not. The seasons are regular and unchanged. The tide ebbs and flows. The earth gives out its abundance to supply man's wants. Who, then, can be insensible to the claim the Great Ruler of all has on us for these favors received?

I now direct your attention to the fittings of the interior of this lodge. You are surrounded with things, the meaning of which you are at present ignorant of; but, as every object here has a hidden truth contained within it, they will be gradually unfolded to you, so that whenever the object is presented to the mind's eyes in ordinary life, you will at once revert to the moral lesson contained in it. Our emblems are scorned by the world, and when exposed to public view, are made the subjects of derision; but to the mind of our brotherhood, they convey instructions that are hidden from those who are uninitiated. The further uses will be communicated in special lodges of instruction.

In order that you may be recognized among brothers, I shall now impart the grip, which is to be given with caution, and only on proof being first given by the party claiming to be recognized.

The grip is (a).

The password is (b).

The universal sign is given with the (c).

This is all the instruction you can at present receive; you will, therefore, take your seat, which I hope to see you occupy for many years, with health and advantage to yourself and family.

N.G.M. - Grand and Subordinate officers and Brothers, before I proceed to close the lodge, let the dues be collected, for which purpose let the Almoner and Recorder wait on each brother and receive their offerings to the cause of Charity, and may you all, out of the substance God has blessed you with, give liberally. The A.G.M. will read the sentences from the Offertory, while the donations are being made.

(The Almoner counts the amount, and the Recorder notes the same. The

Almoner lays the sum on the altar.)

Almoner - We dedicate this free-will offering to the cause of Charity and the necessities of this lodge.

A.G.M. - Let the Doxology be sung - Brothers upstanding. "Praise God from whom all blessings flow," etc.

N.G.M. - Nothing now remains to be done but to treasure up in our minds the beauties of Brotherly Love, and to unite in acts of Fidelity toward one another, and may God's blessing rest on us all. Gr. Warden, you have my commands to close this lodge.

G.W. - I notify you all that the next regular meeting of this lodge will be held on _____, at 4'o clock P.M. Fail not to attend, unless public or private duties to prevent, under our proper displeasure.

(N.G.M. knocks twice and closes.)

RULES TO BE OBSERVED IN THE ARCANA OR DEGREE LODGES

All the G.L Officers to wear white surplices, with purple scarfs over the left shoulder, and aprons bound with the color of the degree., and in the Blue and Pink degrees, sashes of these colors over the right shoulder, crossing on the breast. In the Degree of Fidelity, the purple sash to be dispenses with, and a gold-colored sash only worn. No cloaks or any mask to be worn in a degree work. Brothers to wear blue sashes over the right shoulder; aprons and jewels for past officers, or under dispensation. All lodge to have the means of obscuring the lights when required.

White or Covenant Degree

(N.G.M. strike once; all upstanding.)

N.G.M. - Assist me to open in this Degree.

N.G.M. - Worthy V.G.M., as a Patriot, what do you conceive our duty to be?

V.G.M. - To cultivate the minds of or brothers.

N.G.M. - How do you propose to accomplish this?

V.G.M. - By gradual education.

N.G.M. - What is education?

V.G.M. - Instructions given, which lead, by easy stages, to the acquirement of knowledge.

N.G.M. - On what principles are we met to-night?

V.G.M. - In brotherly love and friendship.

N.G.M. - What is the lecture of the night?

V.G.M. - To teach our brothers what real friendship is.

N.G.M. - Right glad am I to find that our rule prescribes this pleasing occupation. Before I declare this Degree open for conferring the Covenant; our G.W. will receive the Grip and Password of the Covenant from all present.

G.W. *(If all is right)* - The brothers now assembled have proved good and true.

N.G.M. - I have received the report of the G.W., which is satisfactory, and request that our A.G.M. will invoke a blessing on our proceedings. *(All to kneel).*

A.G.M. - O! God, most Holy Creator of all things, by whose Almighty power we live, move, and have our being, we reverently approach Thee, and ask Thy blessing on the means we adopt to instruct one another to look from Nature up to Nature's God. Amen. *(Resume your seats.)*

N.G.M. - Brothers, we are met, this evening, to confer the Covenant Degree on Brother_____, who has petitioned to be permitted to participate in the benefits conferred in this Degree. You will, by your vote, say yes or no. *(If no objection.)*

N.G.M. - Grand Warden, will you see to the candidate, that he is properly prepared for this Degree?

The candidate is to have his wrists bound by a shackle. G.W. brings the candidate to the lodge room door, knocks once.)

G.G. - There is an alarm, N.GM.

N.G.M. - See to the cause,

G.G. *(Opens the wicket and reports)* - Our G.W. and Brother_____ seek admission, and I vouch that your commands have been attended to.

N.G.M. - Let them be admitted.

(The door being opened, the Conductors receive the candidate from the G.W., and conduct him to the front of the altar saying:)

Con. - By the commands of the N.G.M., we introduce Bro. _____ for special instruction in the principles that Patriots should practice to entitle them to Covenant rank.

N.G.M. - I will attend to your wishes. Brother _____, what is your emblematical name?

Answer - (d).

N.G.M. - What do you infer from this? Consider!

Answer - That as he was created in the image of God, and we, his descendants, bear the impress, we should strive to live to honor God.

N.G.M. - Very good, brother. What do you consider your duty to be, seeing that our first parent, who was created and endowed with mental gifts, superior to all other created beings, lost the benefit of his Maker's gift (immortality)?

Answer - I have been so taught, and our everyday experience confirms the truth that mortality is our common lot, and although by the curse that resulted from our first parents' disobedience, we earn our food by the sweat of the brow, it lead to a promise that a Redeemer for mankind should be sent, and from His instructions we learn what course to pursue to regain the happy immortality. This is taught in the unerring standard of Divine Truth, and its practical exhibition consists of "loving thy neighbor as thyself," or doing to others that we would wish others to do to us, if similar posited. *(Conducted, here, to the V.G.M., who continues the theme.)*

V.G.M - This being the case, our duty in this life will be to learn to live so that we may not fear to die; but you must remember that there are many obligations, and as we cannot all see alike, you will have to guard against many things that at first sight may seem contrary to your own opinions. But I tell you, brother, it is this that contracts our sphere of uselessness. It fills the world with sects and parties, who are each one saying, mentally, give place -- my opinions are superior to yours; but you, as an Odd Fellow (which really means that you are singled out from the general mass with a desire for true knowledge), should learn to look beyond the surface, and view with a friendly eye, all mankind. Remember, if some appear vicious in conduct, they are only what you might have been, but for some fortunate circumstance that carried you above its fatal influence; and in like manner, look not with envy upon those who are raised above you in the scale of society. But rather apply yourself to the search, after true knowledge, which will fit you to advance when the time arrives. Thus, when you are able to look on the mean and vile with pity, unmixed with condemnation, and on the high and mighty without envy or malice, then you will have advanced to a condition of things that will secure to you peace of mind, and good will toward all mankind, and will enable you to contemplate your end with that peace that the profligate can never enjoy, and fit you to exalt the password, of this degree, which is (c).

(Conductors again introduce the candidate to the N.G.M., saying:)

Con. - We are desired, by the V.G.M, to introduce Brother _____ for further instructions in this degree.

N.G.M. - My youngest brother, our V.G.M. has put you in possession of the password of the Covenant; he has called your attention to the various phases through which man sees his fellow man pass in the world, and from the attention you appear to have paid to the address just concluded, I infer that you thoroughly estimate the intention of the teachings of this degree. Your initiation and its emblematic trials were intended to teach Brotherly Love, and this Degree, Friendship. I will now release your hands from the shackles, to enable you to salute the brothers of this Degree with the grip of Friendship which I will now communicate to you. The grip is: (f).

N.G.M. -You will now, in company with the G.W., make the circuit of the lodge, and give and receive the grip from every brother in the lodge.

(On returning to the altar, the N.G.M. says:)

N.G.M. - Brother _____, you have made the acquaintance of every brother in the lodge, and henceforth you will be required to speak graciously of the lodge and brothers. Before I can proceed further, I ask you Brother _____, if you are willing to bind yourself by the obligation of an oath to render your fidelity to this Order more binding on your conscience? *(Answer, Yes.)*

N.G.M. - Kneel before the altar, and repeat after me:

I, _____, in the presence of this august assembly, do most solemnly and sincerely promise and swear, with heart in hand, the emblem of this degree, that I will never improperly reval, or lightly talk of the laws and customs of this Order. I will act with True Friendship and Brotherly Love toward every member of this Degree, and will, to the best of my ability, aid and assists every brother proving himself to be such, by administering to his wants according to my means, under the severe penalty of having my eyes thrust out, and being deprived of the means of seeing the beauties of creation, or looking on the face of a friend. All this I devoutly wish--so help me Heaven, and keep me steadfast to fulfill my promise.

(The obligation is sealed, by the candidate kissing the Book of Sacred Law twice.)

N.G.M. *(Taking the brother's hand with the grip)* - Rise, brother Covenanted Odd Fellow. I requested the G.W. will remove Brother_____'s apron, and clothe him with the proper badge of the Covenant.

(An apron 12 inches square, and upper fall 4 inches at the apex, with a blue and white rosette fixed in the centre, is put on.)

G.W. - Brother_____, I now clothe you with the badge of the Covenant Degree; you observe that one rosette is fixed on the upper flap. It signifies singleness of purpose, or True Friendship, being the social tie that binds you to one another. N.G.M., your commands are obeyed.

N.G.M. - Brother_____, the first emblem of this Degree is the (g). It is highly prized by every Odd Fellow. It exhibits that the heart should be ready to accompany the hand when given in Friendship. The value of wealth is light as air compared with the value of a true friend, as regards human happiness - for, remember, money may purchase apparent comforts, but a genuine friend is above the purchase by sordid treasure. Our A.G.M. will unfold to you the practical results of this divine gift. Scene Supporters, make all things ready. Brother____, bow down and commune with thyself; place your hand over your eye, and shut out all external objects.

(The room is to be darkened, and the meeting of David and Jonathan takes the place of the death scene. All being ready the A.G.M. touches the brother with a white hand.)

A.G.M. - Arise, brother, from your meditation, and contemplate the scene before you. This is one of the many results of Friendship, of which Holy Writ informs us. The tale is very instructive. David, a shepherd boy, left his father's flocks, to carry a gift to the camp of Saul, the King of Israel, in whose army his three elder brothers were serving; and toward the Israelites, defying them to fight in single combat, and cursing the God of Israel. This caused the indignation of David, and he longed to take away the reproach east on his nation. He offered his services to the King and was accepted, and with a sling and a stone, slew the giant, Goliath. He rose, in consequence, to public favor, which displeased King Saul, who had offered his daughter in marriage to the victor. The King appeared to be friendly to him, while he hated him in heart, and sought, on more than one occasion, to take his life. This is the picture of counterfeit friendship, and requires your utmost care to guard against its snares. The open enemy is far less dangerous than the false friend.

A.G.M. - The opposite quality is exhibited in the conduct of Jonathan, the son of King Saul, of whom it is said: "Jonathan loved David as his own soul;" and he entered into a covenant with him, and in token, he stripped himself of his robe, his under garments, his sword, his bow and his girdle, and gave them to David. We infer from this that True Friendship, in like manner, divests itself of self, and virtually says: all that I have, I devote to your requirements, if necessity should call on me to do so. Brother, Scripture tells you that your duty to mankind is to "love thy neighbor as thyself;" not better than yourself; therefore it not required of you, as far as worldly affairs are concerned, to deprive of yourself, or those near and dear to you by family ties, of their home comforts, to spend them on Friendship, but only to minister as far as you can to the general wants of the distressed of mankind. The case of Jonathan, already stated, was an extreme one, and we find many, in the height of their zeal, ready and willing, on the impulse of the moment, to do that which they regret afterward. This results, sometimes, from principles imperfectly formed. Jonathan was one of those bright and scarce examples that allowed Friendship to occupy the first place in his affections; and when placed against family interests (in which the policy too often is to sacrifice friendship to support it), he, with stern integrity of purpose, resolved to do his duty. The details are to be found in the 20th chapter of the 1st Book of Samuel, which I will read for your instruction. (*Goes to the altar and reads by the aid of a taper.*)

A.G.M. - You have now heard the narrative; lay the instructions to heart, and always do your duty to your friend, when you have proved him as such, and leave the issue with God.

(*On the lodge being restored to light, the A.G.M. gives the sign of the Covenant, which is done by (h).*)

This explains the meaning of the second emblem. The third is the (i), and exhibits the strength of Friendship when the true bond of

David and Jonathan entered into a covenant of friendship. Jonathan warned David of his father's murderous intentions. He went to his father and pleaded not to harm David.

Brotherly Love binds us together, and the weakness of any cause when undertaken single handed, trusting in our own strength.

N.G.M. - In following up the remarks of the A.G.M., by way of conclusion, reflect well on the importance of the step you have taken, which I hope has impressed on your mind the value, power, and necessity of Friendship, which teaches us to meet together as brethren, and thus become mutually interested in each other's welfare. Lay the instructions to heart, and seek to practically realize what Brotherly Love, strengthened by Friendship, will accomplish. Brother_____, these are all the instructions we have to impart; you will resume your seat, while I prepare to close this Degree.

(The A.G.M. will offer the closing prayer.)

A.G.M. - Oh! Thou, Giver of all good, grant us grace to utter acceptable thanks for all the mercies that have attended us hitherto, and grant, most holy Father, that we may love only for Thy hoor, to our life's end. Amen.

N.G.M. - Brothers, upstanding, and assist me to close this Degree Lodge - each giving the sign of the Covenant. G.W., you have my commands to close this lodge.

G.W. - By command of the N.G.M., I declare this Covenant Degree closed, and to be opened again this day, four months.

N.G.M. - Our labors in this Degree being ended, let us depart in peace, and may God bless us all.

Royal Blue Degree

(The Office Bearers being in their places, the N.G.M. strikes twice.)

N.G.M. - I shall proceed to open the Royal Blue Degree. Worthy V.G.M, are you ready to commence the work?

V.G.M. - I am ever ready to obey the N.G.M.'s commands.

N.G.M. -What instruction does the Royal Blue degree impart?

V.G.M. -The Love of the Brotherhood.

N.G.M. - This subject is worthy of the research of all wise men. Let the Gr. Warden receive the grip and password of this Degree from all present. *(If satisfied, to report:)*

G.W. - The brothers are proved correct.

N.G.M. - Before we proceed to the work, let the A.G.M. invoke a blessing.

A.G.M. - Immaculate and Holy Ruler of all things, look down with infinite mercy on us; kindle in our hearts a feeling of Love which shall reflect that divine attribute upon all who come in contact with us. Amen.

N.G.M. - We are met this evening to receive the petition of Brother_____, who desires further instructions in the principles and precepts of our Order. You will, by your votes, say yea or nay. *(If no objection, to proceed.)*

N.G.M. - The G.W. and Conductors will retire and introduce the brother in proper form.

(The G.W. examines the brother in former Degrees, and knocks twice.)

G.G. - There is an alarm.

N.G.M. - See to the cause. *(The cause reported.)*

G.G. - At the door of the lodge, stands Brother_____, under safe Conductors, who has been received in the lodge with fraternal affection, instructed in the work of True Friendship, and now wishes for further instructions in the mystery of Odd Fellowship.

N.G.M. - Let him be admitted and conducted to the V.G.M.

Con. - Our N.G.M. has directed us to introduce to your notice Brother _____, who craves instructions in the Royal Blue Degree.

V.G.M. - Your request shall be attended to; but I must first examine the candidate in his previous degrees, to ascertain whether he is worthy to receive increased knowledge.

(The candidate is examined in the Signs, Passwords and Grips of the Making and Covenant Degrees.)

V.G.M. - Having proved to me that former instructions have not been wasted on you, I shall proceed to instruct you in the claims the Brotherhood now have on you. I shall as briefly as possible inform you that the subject to which your attention will be directed, is that all important one of the Love of the Brotherhood. Odd Fellowship is intended to teach and carry into practical operation the immutable truth that the great human family are the brothers; that we ought to cherish brotherly feelings toward every member of society, be their rank what it may. We are not to stop short to consider the nostrums of contending sects or parties, but to promote man's comforts by proselyting them to our principles, independently of such considerations. In this development consists the true dignity of the Order-*Brotherly Love;* whose development will extend our influence beyond the reach of condemnation.

The Password of the Degree is *(j)*.

V.G.M. - Conduct the candidate to the N.G.M.

Con. - We are desired by the V.G.M. to introduce Brother _____, for further instructions in the Royal Blue Degree.

N.G.M. - Brother_____, the password of this Degree must furnish me the text of my address. The moral law or Ten Commandments refer to our outward acts, and the Levitical Law demands an eye for an eye, a tooth for a tooth, but the lesson taught in the New Testament by the Lord of Life was: "See that ye love one another;" and St. John, in his beautiful epistles, says: "He that saith he is in light and hateth his brother, is in darkness; but he that loveth his brother is in light, and there is no occasion for stumbling in him;" and again: "He that hateth his brother is in darkness, and knoweth not whither he goeth." These texts are worth a life-long consideration. Think what life would be without love. Think of the dark catalogue of crimes, if hatred were the general rule, in place of the exception. To counteract this evil, it becomes imperative that we should strive to cultivate Love for one another, and as members of one great Family regard the interests of the brotherhood as inseparable from our own. If we do so, with greater gratification can we experience than when we gladden the sick chamber by our visits, console the dying brother with words of comfort, or carry aid to the bereft widow and fatherless orphan. Love is a sentiment that is co-extensive with Friendship, from which it primarily springs, and yet underlays its basis. We are taught "to love our enemies and to do good to them who despitefully use you." These injunctions are hard to understand, but we devoutly receive them as truths. But the Love of the Brotherhood we should all endeavor to make ourselves practically conversant with.

In order that the subject of this Degree may be deeply impressed on your mind, a further vow of Fidelity is required to you. Kneel before the Word of Truth, and repeat after me:

I, _____, in this conclave of brothers, promise and swear to uphold the principles of Brotherly Love in word and deed. I will as far as in my power lies assist with food, raiment or advice, all true brothers of this Degree, on proof of worthiness; and if I deny him when I have the means by me, may I be branded with infamy as a perjured man, unworthy of further consideration. All this I swear, or suffer the penalty of having molten lead poured into my ears, and thus cut off hearing the sound of the human voice, which cheers and elevates man above all other created things.

N.G.M - Kiss the book of sacred law thrice. Brother, kneel and lay thy head in thy hands and reflect on what thou hast heard.

(*While reflecting, the lodge is darkened, and the scene of the Good Samaritan prepared in the usual place. The N.G.M. then takes a cup made in the form of a heart, open at the top, into which spirit is poured, which is lighted, and then he says:*)

N.G.M - Arise, my Royal Brother, and by the light of this emblem of Love receive a change of clothing to denote your rank.

(*The G.W removes the covenant apron and ties on the apron of this Degree.*)

G.W. - I clothe you with the emblem of this Degree. It is an apron bound with a blue binding., which denotes that you are now bound to the Brotherhood by vows of Fidelity of a threefold character, viz: Fraternity, strengthened by Friendship., and cemented by Love.

A.G.M. - My son, turn thine eyes this way, and tell me what

The parable of the Good Samaritan teaches people to be charitable even to a needy stranger.

thou seest?

Candidate - I see a figure of a man apparently dying, and another administering to his wants.

A.G.M. - This scene is intended to represent the parable of the Good Samaritan, and I cannot do better than read the instructive narrative to you. *(Reads Tenth chapter of St. Luke.)*

A.G.M. - Learn from this parable who was the neighbor to the afflicted and distressed. The Priest, the Levite, and the Good Samaritan, represent different grades of humanity. The Priest represents the class of persons who on hearing the tale of woe pretend to have great sympathy with the sufferer, and are very loud with advice of what ought to be done: but, nevertheless, give no practical effect to their advice by a gift. The Good Samaritan exhibits a class of philanthropic persons who never stops to inquire from what cause distress has arisen, but at once relieves in a practical manner the wants; or, in other words, pour wine and oil on the wound. My son, imitate the conduct of the Good Samaritan. Consider that if at any time your bounties have been abused by the artifices of some despicable wretch, whose conscience will be his greatest tormentor, you have discharged your duty as taught by the Order in the Degree of Brotherly Love.

The sign of this Degree is given by *(k)*. The grip is given by *(l)*.

The principal emblem of this Degree is *(m)*; from this we learn the Love that God had for man when the sacrifice of the Lord for our sins was required to procure our salvation.

The Dove and Olive Branch we recognize as the emblem of Peace and Love, and brings to mind that when destruction came down on this world in the form of a deluge, Noah and his family were saved as the representatives of a better state.

The two Rods of Moses and Aaron exhibit in one case that God's love will provide a remedy when all human external aid seems to fail. Thus Hored struck, gave drink to the famished Israelites; and in the other case, it exhibit that God's love is often shown in chastisement and that while the families of Korah, Dathan, and Abiram, were swallowed up for rebellion against God's High Priest, by this severe punishment the rest of the people were saved from their sin.

Learn from this that although distress and troubles may bear heavily on you, it will teach you humility, and enable you to feel for the distressed in the hour of affliction and the time of need. This ends the Royal Blue Degree; resume your seat.

N.G.M. - Before I close this Degree, the A.G.M. will offer up prayer.

PRAYER

A.G.M. - Most Holy and infinite God, thy omnipotence and omniscience we adore. Thy power and knowledge fill our hearts with humility. Thou knowest our wants and desires before we know them ourselves. Nature, by Thy command, provides for our daily wants. Inspire our hearts with divine Love through the influence of Thy holy will, that purity and devotion may forever influence our future lives. Amen.

N.G.M. - Grand Warden, you have my command to close this Degree; let each brother be upstanding, giving the Royal Sign *(k.)*

G.W. - By command of the N.G.M, I declare this Royal Blue Degree Lodge closed until this day, four months.

N.G.M - Our duty in this Degree being concluded, let us depart in peace.

Pink or Merit Degree

(In this Degree, the lodge should be arranged in the usual order. The elective officers, both past and present, to wear the emblem of their official rank over the right shoulder, and a pink sash over the left shoulder, crossing on the breast, and all taking part in the ceremonial to be armed with Templars' swords. N.G.M. knocks with the handle of his sword three times, saying:)

N.G.M. - Brothers, assist me to open this lodge in the Fourth Degree.

(All upstanding, leaning on their swords.)

N.G.M. - Worthy V.G.M., what do the rules of our fraternity teach us?

V.G.M. - To be Just and True.

N.G.M. - What is Justice?

V.G.M. - The rights that every brother of this lodge should receive at our hands.

N.G.M. - What is Truth?

V.G.M. - The only object worthy of the research of the truly wise.

N.G.M. - Since this is the case, officers and brothers, let justice occupy our attention, both practically and theoretically, this night.

(The petitions of any candidates are now to be read, and a report made of their proficiency in the former Degrees, and if they are satisfactory, the votes are to be collected, and if favorable, the G.W. is to strike three times with the handle of his sword.)

G.G. - There is an alarm.

N.G.M. - See to the cause.

G.G. - There is at the door of the lodge Brother_____, who comes under safe conduct, has been received with fraternal affection, instructed in the true principles of True Friendship, cemented by

Love, and now seeks for further instructions in the moral precepts of the Order.

N.G.M. - The brothers will attend the candidate with drawn swords, in procession, once round the lodge room, and when the candidate is placed before the V.G.M., form a circle round him, elevating your swords over his head, the points to culminate so as to form the roof of steel. When the candidate is in the proper position, the V.G.M. shall examine the brother in his former Degrees.

(The responses being given, the V.G.M. says:)

V.G.M. - Brother_____, what do you require?

Candidate - Justice.

V.G.M. - What do you conceive justice to be?

Candidate - The reward of my merit.

V.G.M. - Brother _____, you have made a very fatal demand, for if your merits are to be weighed in the scales of the sanctuary, you will assuredly be found wanting, and death must be the result. You are now surrounded by armed men, to whom you must prove that at least you have some claim to support the demand you have made. Give us briefly an account of yourself, that we may judge of your merits.

Candidate -I have given myself up to search after true knowledge, which our A.G.M. has informed me to know myself. I have applied the lessons of instruction to practice, and discovered that Friendship and Brotherly Love is the only real foundation on which human happiness can be based. Having, as far as possible, practically carried these principles out in my daily communications with the brotherhood, I thought I had a fair title to claim merit for what I had accomplished by my example and precept, and, in this belief, I asked for justice in recognition of what I had done.

V.G.M. - Brother_____, you have erred in judgment in doing so; but as you seem to have profited by the instructions you have already received, and are determined to still persevere in the search of wisdom, I will take it upon myself to acquit you of presumption. Companions, sheath your swords, resume your places in the lodge, and leave the candidate with me for further instructions. Brother_____, you state that your mind has grasped the truths of Friendship and

Brotherly Love, and your aspirations are for further knowledge, and in your zeal you have asked for justice. Know, my brother, that justice, to be useful in this world, must be combined with charity, in order that it may be counterbalanced; for you must know that when power is vested in man, his prejudices often prevent him from doing justice; his decisions are warped by selfishness. Remember, brother, if you should be called on to judge between brother and brother, in the execution of our laws, seek to divest yourself of all prejudice or partiality, giving latitude for the zealous, and bearing with the weakness of our fellowmen, and by your decision seek to bring them back to the path of rectitude, in place of driving them from you. Let me, therefore, say, judge with candor, and reprehend with mercy. I shall now give you the password of this Degree; it is (n). Conduct the candidate to the N.G.M.

Con. - We are requested by the V.G.M. to present Brother _____ to you in the name of justice, for further instructions in this Degree.

N.G.M. - My brother, your desire for instruction has rendered you guilty of presumption. Know that justice and equity are reflections of divine attributes, and in our human existence are only capable of being faintly reflected and judged of by comparison. Remember, if your demand for justice could have been fairly tested by your fellow-man, you would have had to show that you deserved it, and to prove this, you must have been faultless; that you had never in word, thought or deed, injured anyone; for you must bear in mind, that however much you may regret an evil deed, or repent of injury done, it does not remove the crime. Hence, all men are more or less guilty, and are not in a position to demand justice, in the real sense of the word. This consideration must teach humility to us all, and while endeavoring to be just and good to all mankind, we must be ever ready to bear and forbear--remembering that when our tempers are tried by the taunts of the worthless, that the wise King of Israel says: "A soft word turneth away wrath; but grievous words stirreth up anger." Brother _____, you are now in the conclave of brothers, asking for instructions in the paths of virtue. Let your future conduct prove that you have benefited by the teachings of the Merit Degree. I now demand from you a further promise. Kneel before the Divine Law, and repeat after me:

I, _____, in the presence of this assembly, with the prospect of the great judgment in my mind, do most solemnly promise and swear that, avoiding all evil thoughts and acts toward the brothers of the

Merit Degree, I will, as far as my example and authority will permit, seek to carry out in my daily occupation the precepts of the Degree of Merit, and if I swerve from the teachings, willfully, and injure my brother in malice, may the power of speech be taken from me, that I may become dumb before my accusers, and an object of contempt to every Patriot. In token of which, I bow in reverence, and kiss the Holy Law four times.

(The brother is to be kept kneeling, while the room is darkened, and the Conductors produce the transparency of Brutus delivering his son up to justice.)

N.G.M. - Arise, Brother _____, and reflect on the scene before you. Think what this Pagan chief did to the honor of justice, and think what you are required to do if you wish to walk uprightly in this world. We all have our besetting sins that attach themselves to us; when you have discovered the sin, be firm, strong and steady, to deliver it up to justice, and thus you will gain the respect of all good men, and the peace of mind resulting from an approving conscience. Brother _____, I shall request the G.W. to invest you with the clothing of this Degree.

G.W. - By desire of the N.G.M., I invest you with a similar apron to that given in the Royal Blue Degree, but it is adorned with one rosette, on the upper flap, denoting singleness of purpose. I crown you with a chaplet of laurel, in token of the victory you have won over your evil habits. A four-fold tie now binds you to our fraternity, viz: Brotherly Love, with Truth, Friendship and Justice, combined.

(The A.G.M. reads the first five verses of the seventh chapter of St. Matthew, and says:)

A.G.M. -Reflect, my son, on the words recorded by the Holy Evangelist. Let them sink deep into your heart; let them be the guide of your life, and then your last days will be crowned with everlasting peace.

The sign of this Degree is given by *(o)*.

The grip is given by *(p)*.

The emblems belonging to this Degree are *(q).;* and are intended to represent the weighing of our good and evil actions in the Scales of Truth, the judging of them by the Laws of God, and the

The Scales of Truth and Sword of Justice

determination to sacrifice our evil habits by the Sword of Justice.

N.G.M. - *(Then to give four knocks, saying:)* Brothers, assist me to close this Degree; be upstanding, giving the sign of the Merit Degree.

A.G.M. - Great Creator of all things, bless the means we use in impressing the minds of those assembled here this night with their duty toward the Most High and their fellow-men. Amen.

G.W. - Our labors in this Degree being ended, I declare this Degree Lodge closed until this night, three months.

The Arch of Titus was erected by the Senate and people of Rome in memory of the Emperor Titus. It has been claimed that the present name "Odd Fellows" was given by Titus Caesar in 79 A.D., who from the singularity of their notions and from their knowing each other by night or by day, and from their fidelity to him and their country, not only gave them such name but, at the same time as a pledge of friendship, presented them a charter, engraved on a plate of gold, bearing different emblems - such as the sun, moon, stars, the lamb, the lion, the dove and other emblems of mortality.

Royal Arch of Titus or Fidelity Degree

(The lodge room to be fitted with great care. The A.G.M., the N.G.M., and the V.G.M, to wear gold colored sashes over the left shoulder; black aprons, and black gloves. They shall stand in the South, East and West, with a sceptre in their right hand, thus occupying the three points of an equilateral triangle, intersecting the other. The G. Guardian to be within the lodge. When these seven are in proper position, the Degree shall be commenced as follows:)

A.G.M. - My Excellent Companions, we are assembled, this evening, to renew our solemn vows, and to certify that such is our desire, let each give the sign of Fidelity *(r)*.

(While this is done, the three sceptres are to be laid on the altar, from whence the A.G.M. must take the Book of Sacred Law and kiss it, handing it to the N.G.M. It is then passed to the whole in rotation, when the G.T. shall return the Book of Sacred Law to its place, and the principals shall resume their sceptres.)

A.G.M. - In whose presence are we met tonight?

N.G.M. - In the presence of the Holy One of Israel, who must not be named with unhallowed lips. Let the A.G.M., letter the sacred name, that we, as the seven principals, may recognize the same: A.G.M., *J.*; N.G.M., *E.*; V.G.M., *H.*; G.W., *O.*; G.S., *V.*; G.T., *A.*; G.G., *H.*

(The lettering is to be commenced in rotation by each in turn, until the sacred name has been rendered complete by each. A basin of pure water and a flagon of wine shall be placed on the altar. The A.G.M shall rinse his hands and wipe with a napkin, and each in succession shall do the same. The A.G.M. shall take the loving cup and drink, saying:

A.G.M. - "In His Holy name I pledge you all."

(Each having done the same, the lodge is to be opened, as follows:)

A.G.M – My son, it is well that we have met to renew our vows; therefore take your position in the East, and let the Grand Officers take their proper situations, while you open the lodge.

N.G.M. – How many members must be present to complete a Lodge of Fidelity?

A.G.M. – Seven.

N.G.M. – Why seven?

A.G.M. – Because it is a sacred number. Thus seven days were assigned to Creation. Seven spirits are before the throne of God. The candlestick had seven branches as a holy symbol. Seven Churches represented extensions of the doctrine of the cross in its various stages, and the seven dispensations that have governed mankind from Creation.

N.G.M. – How do you make that appear?

A.G.M. – Adam in paradise was in a state of holy innocence. Enoch represented the antediluvian age, and his holy life caused him to be translated to Heaven, having testified through a long life against the wickedness of the generations who called themselves the sons of God, on whom the mighty deluge came. Abraham represented the age of Faith and Promise, and was selected to be the great progenitor of the Jewish nation, to whom was entrusted the keeping of the Holy Law. Joshua represented the age of the Judges, and acted under the influence of a Divine Theocracy. Samuel, called by the Lord to inaugurate a prophetic dispensation, and by divine command anointed David to be the visible King of the Church Militant, and his successors were rulers in the world until Jesus Christ was born, whose kingdom was to be set-up in the hearts of mankind, and to have no end, being a spiritual dominion, and under these holy influences we are met this night.

N.G.M. – With deep humility, lay your hands on your hearts, while the A.G.M. invokes a blessing on this assembly. Companions, bow to the East, and listen to the prayer of the A.G.M.

A.G.M. – Oh! Thou Great Infinite, Self-existent Spirit! The very contemplation of Thy perfections renders our efforts to serve Thee the vanity. It is as the glimmer of the twilight compared with the sun in meridian splendor. Our best aspirations would be but worthless, but for the hope which Thou has implanted in us through the revelations of Divine Truth, taught by the blessed Redeemer of mankind. We bow Thee in deep humility. Amen.

N.G.M. – I declare this Lodge of Fidelity open for the purpose of conferring the Degree of the Royal Arch of Titus.

(Seven knocks to be given by the three Chief Officers, and the Guardian to strike seven times on the lodge door.)

N.G.M. –Worthy Grand Guardian, you are now directed to admit all who are waiting that can give the sign and password to the G.W., who will pass into the ante-room to vouch for them.

(When all are admitted and seated, the G.S. shall read the minutes of the last meeting; on the same day being confirmed, the lodge proceed to business. The G.S. then to report that the candidates have signed petitions. The petitions shall be read, the N.G.M. shall say:)

N.G.M. – Excellent Companions, Brother_____ has petitioned to be exalted to the highest privileges our Sublime Order recognizes; The G.W. will collect the votes.

(All being found correct)

N.G.M. – Let the candidate be robed in the garment of innocence, vailed with humility, his feet bare, a pilgrim's staff in his left hand. Let the Companions take their wands and arrange themselves in two rows from East to West, facing each other.

(The candidate is to be prepared for the ceremony as follows: His coat, hat and shoes are to be removed; a white robe to be placed on his person, covering him to the feet; a black cloth to be placed over his head, and thus led to the door of the lodge. The six Grand Officers are each to approach the altar where the Holy Law is lying, the A.G.M. saying:)

A.G.M. – May our minds be enlightened from this divine source of Truth.

(*And taking a small lamp intended to represent the light of Faith, pour perfumed oil into the same, and having ignited it, all the other lights in the room are to be extinguished. When the perfume of incense has permeated the lodge room, the candidate is to be admitted as follows: The G.W. having appointed a qualified Companion to act as Almoner, he announces the candidate, places the pilgrim's staff in his left hand, and taking his right, knocks seven times on the door.*)

G.G. – Most Noble Grand Master, a Companion announces himself by the sacred number.

N.G.M. – Look well to the portal, and report who it is.

G.G. – Our Almoner, in company with what appears to be a Pilgrim in search of Wisdom, and claims admittance to the lodge.

N.G.M. – As the Almoner bears him company, let them be admitted and brought to our presence by the proper number of steps.

(*The door being opened, the candidate is conducted by the seven steps to the West end of the room, and order to kneel down*).

A.G.M. – Oh, most High and Omnipotent Ruler of all things; inspire our lips with wisdom to enable us to impart true knowledge to the candidate who now kneels before Thee. Amen.

N.G.M. – Brother_____, how came you here, and what do you desire from us?

Candidate – N.G.M., I come here to petition for further instruction in the principles in which our Order is founded.

N.G.M. – That being the case, let the candidate be brought by seven further steps to the altar. (*Being brought to the altar*)

N.G.M. – Brother _____, you have now entered the sanctum of our Order by fourteen steps, of which I will, in proper time, inform you the meaning; but I will, at this stage, I shall proceed to examine you in your proficiency in the former Degrees of Instruction, in order that I may prove if you are worthy to be entrusted with further knowledge of the character of the Order.

N.G.M. – Who was the founder of the human race?

Candidate – Adam.

N.G.M. – What does the name remind you of?

Candidate – Our lowly origin.

N.G.M. – Give me the sign and password of the Initiatory Degree.

Candidate – (*Gives the sign and password*).

N.G.M. – What further progress have you made in the Order?

Candidate – I have the White and Covenant Degree.

N.G.M. – What does the Degree teach us?

Candidate – The principles of Friendship.

N.G.M. – Can you give me the Grip of the Covenant?

Candidate – I can. (*Gives it*).

N.G.M. – What did the Covenant Degree lead to?

Candidate – The Royal Blue Degree.

N.G.M. – What does the Royal Blue Degree teach?

Candidate – Brotherly Love.

N.G.M. – Have you any other test of merit?

Candidate – My attainments rendered me worthy to receive the Pink or Merit Degree.

N.G.M. – What is the password of the Merit Degree?

Candidate – (*Gives it*).

N.G.M. – Your answers prove to me that you have paid attention to the lessons of instruction already imparted, and encourage me to continue the task, to enable you to disseminate the principles of mortality among within those with whom you associate in the daily walks of life. I call on you to kneel and enter into a solemn compact before the assembled Companions, that you will be faithful unto death: Kneel down, lay the pilgrim's staff on the rights side, place both hands on the Book of Sacred Law before you, and repeat after me:

I, _____, do most sincerely promise and swear in this Lodge of Fidelity, in the presence of my brother Companions, that will all things prove myself worthy of the confidence reposed in me. I will in all my dealings, endeavor to promote the influence of this Order, the Judeo-Christian religion, the peace of the Realm, the honor of the reigning Monarch, and the Constitution of the Kingdom, with singleness of heart. I further promise, that I will not retain as friends any who declare defiance a strict regard for virtue and morality, even though they may cost me the pain of severing the natural ties of blood; keeping in mind the saying of the Savior of mankind, that "he that loveth father or mother more than me is not worthy of me." I bind myself by the dread of eternal death and the future judgment to fulfill, as far as my human nature will permit, this, my solemn promise, in token of which I kiss this Book of Sacred law seven times.

N.G.M. – Your obligation has now bound you by indissoluble ties to this fraternity and, while the officers prepare to give light to the lodge, take the pilgrim's staff in your right hand, and follow your conductor, making the circuit of triangle twice, occupying fourteen steps in each circuit, stopping at each seven.

(*The candidate is to follow the Almoner, as instructed, while the officers take each lamp, and in succession light their lamps from the sacred light burning on the altar. Then each standing on the apex of the intersected triangle, with the Grand Guardian within the lodge, each with their lamps lit in their hands, the candidate shall be brought up between the Companions, who shall reach their wands across and form an avenue;*

when arrived at the proper place in from of the altar the A.G.M. shall say:)

A.G.M. – Brother_____, you have now entered among Companions who, like yourself, have been led by the love of Peace, Morality and Equity, to study the teachings of the Great Ruler, and are here tonight to receive the reward due to you perseverance. Permit me further to say that none to whom the secrets of this Degree have been entrusted have ever had cause to regret their choice. The good men of all ages have been the Odd Fellows. It has been these Odd Fellows that have stood prominent; whose deeds have been recorded, but you must bear in mind that they rarely received the rewards of their merits in life. Thus we have the example of the first martyr, Abel, whose acceptable sacrifice procured him the ill-will of this brother. Noah, a believer in the word of God, prepared an Ark, in which his family were saved, and was for this act mocked and despised by the generation who lived in his day. Abraham had his trials. Joseph, despised by his brethren, was sold by as a slave. Moses, when worldly honors were presented, chose rather to suffer with his distressed brothers than to be called the son of the Pharaoh's daughter. David was haunted and his life sought after by his own relations, and throughout the world's history, goodness has always received ill-will and opposition of mankind,; and even the blessed Savior of mankind was despitefully used, when his whole life was devoted in going about doing good. Shall we, then, expect aught else if we render ourselves conspicuous by the mode we adopt of bringing about a higher state of morality than is practiced by those with whom we have to contend in the world? Listen to the further instructions of the N.G.M.

N.G.M. – Brother _____, you have listened to the preliminary address of the Ancient Grand Master. I will now direct your attention to the number seven. These are the gradations of life. A man's years are said by the Psalmist to be three-score years and ten, and in passing through this long probation, well will it be if we find true wisdom. The first seven years are infancy; the second seven years, childhood; the third seven years, youth; the fourth, fifth and sixth periods are devoted to adulthood, its care and duties; and the seventh period is the age of the 'sere and yellow leaf,' after which the spirit goes back to the Grand Ruler who gave it, and our material frame returns to the earth, from which we were created.

The number seven relates, also, to the great moral dispensations of this world. First, created Innocence in paradise, holding free intercourse with the Deity. Second, the period of the Descendants of Adam, or the Antedeluvian age. The third, was the Patriarchal Age. The fourth, the Mosaic Age, governed by laws given to the Jewish people from Mount Sinai. The fifth was the Prophetic Age. The sixth, the Regal Period; and the seventh, is the Christian Period, governed by the doctrine: "Do unto others that you wish others to do unto yourselves," and this is the fundamental principle of Odd Fellowship. The first chapter of the Gospel of St. Matthew recounts that six times seven generations were accomplished from the promise made by Abraham, that in his seed all generations of man should be blessed. Thus, fourteen generations elapsed from Abraham to David, the first monarch of the Jews, who reigned in Jerusalem. The next period of fourteen generations was from David to Jechonias, who was carried away captive with the people of Babylon, as a punishment for having deserted their God, and contemned the Holy law committed to their charge; and for seventy years, the symbol of the age of man, they were strangers in the land of the Babylonians, until God in his mercy raised up Cyrus, who ordered a Royal proclamation for the Jews to return to their own land, and returned the gold and silver that at the destruction of the Temple designed by David, but build by Solomon, had been carried away be Nebuchadnezzar. The third period of fourteen generations extended from Jechonias to the blessed Lord and Savior, Jesus Christ, whose name many people adore. It is this reason why you were conducted thrice fourteen steps in the progress of taking this Degree, answering to the number of generations from the call of Abraham to the birth of Christ, the Redeemer of mankind, who sent out his disciples into all lands to preach the Gospel. Those who constituted the Jewish nation saw no beauty in the promised Messiah, of whom both the Law and the Prophets testified, and committed the sin of bearing false witness against him, saying, in reply to Pilate, when he said: I can find no fault in him – away with him, his blood be on us and our children. How fearfully was this fulfilled in their case. Swift destruction came on the nation; the Romans came up against them to crush a rebellion, and they having shut themselves up in Jerusalem for the defense of the Temple, perished miserably by internal dissensions, by famine, by fire and by sword. The Temple was again destroyed; the remnant of the people carried captives to Rome to grace the triumphs of Titus on his return. In honor of this was erected the Royal Arch of

Titus, to which degree you are now raised.

(The officers now move to the head of the two lines of Companions, standing three on a side in a curved line, leaving a space at the top for the key of the Arch. The Almoner is then to place a helmet on the head of the candidate, after removing the vail, sandals on his feet, a breastplate round his neck, a shirt emblazoned with the sign of the Cross on his left arm, his pilgrim's staff taken from him, and a sword substituted. When thus arrayed, the Almoner shall say:)

    Almoner – Companions, here is a Christian in complete armor, willing to take the field against sin and unbelief. What are your wishes?

    N.G.M. – On behalf of the Companions, let me say we wish our lodge to be emblematical of the good intentions of our Order, which cannot exist without the aid of practical Christianity, which is the element that enables us to combine to counteract the wickedness of the world; so let Brother _____ be placed as the Keystone to bind the Royal Arch together.

(The candidate is then moved to the center of the Arch, which has hitherto been vacant, and thus completes the Royal Arch. While in this form, the Almoner to read from the 6th Chapter of the Epistle to the Ephesians, commencing at the 10th and terminating at 18th verse. The Almoner now takes a place in the Arch, and the N.G.M. moves to the center of the column, saying:)

    Almoner – Brother _____, advance to me by seven short steps. *(Candidate does so.)*

    N.G.M. – Brother _____, the lesson you have to learn from the fate of the Jewish nation must be indelibly imprinted on your mind. In the first place, this people were nurtured up in Egypt until their numbers and peculiarity of their actions rendered them objects of mistrust, and led to their oppression; but the Law was with them, and in good time delivered them from their bondage, and led them to the hand of Moses and Joshua to a land flowing with milk and honey. Nevertheless, they forgot their obligations for mercies received, abjured God, and reviled His holy name by worshipping idols of the nations that surrounded them. Transgression and repentances were followed by punishment and deliverances until at last they nationally only retained the outward show of religion, while the spirit was a dead letter. Our blessed Redeemer, looking on the city of Jerusalem, exclaimed: "How oft would I have gathered you as a hen gathereth her chickens under her wings, but you would not, and now you are left desolate." Therefore, the Royal Arch of Titus is left to us as a warning that God will no more dwell with man in Temples reared with hands. Twice it was permitted, and by the sins of those to whom the holy symbols were entrusted, their conduct brought down destruction, and will never again be rebuilt; but now, by the Divine power of God, He will dwell in the men's hearts when they consecrate themselves to do His will on earth, and to this end we hope you will study to serve God, and receive the reward of a holy life by dwelling in a blissful eternity in the regions of joy for evermore.

N.G.M. – I now present you with a sash of gold, as an emblem that as gold is the most precious of metals, an Odd Fellow should one of the best of men. The sign of this Degree is never to be given out of the lodge. It consists of (s).

(*The Royal Arch is then reformed, and a procession moves thrice around the lodge room. The Companion at the dexter foot of the column to lead. On the first round, the A.G.M., N.G.M, and V.G.M. leave and take their seats in the East. On the next round, the G.G., G.W., and G. Sec. leave and take their places. On the third round, the Companions will leave their wands in charge of the Grand Guardian at the door, and each salute the N.G.M. on passing, with the sign of this Degree, before resuming their seats. If no further business is to be transacted, the password is to be lettered round the lodge, commencing with the N.G.M., going South, West, and returning to the East. The A.G.M. shall say the benediction. The V.G.M. shall then declare the Degree closed until a warrant is issued to hold the next chapter. All reply Amen.*)

𝔐𝔢𝔯𝔤𝔢𝔯 𝔞𝔫𝔡 𝔖𝔲𝔠𝔠𝔢𝔰𝔰𝔦𝔬𝔫

On January 8, 1798, the *Ancient Order of Odd Fellows* and the *Patriotic Order of Odd Fellows* entered into a merger as the *Grand United Order of Odd Fellows* (GUOOF).[1] The *Gentleman's Magazine of 1798* mentioned that the Original United Lodge of Odd Fellows consisted of 50 lodges, 39 of them in London and its environs." It was also during this time when the Order allegedly abandoned all political and religious disputes and committed itself to promoting the harmony and welfare of its members.

However, miscommunication led some lodges in the Manchester area to declare themselves independent from the United Order in 1810 and organized themselves as the *Manchester Unity Independent Order of Odd Fellows* (MUIOOF) in 1813. The Manchester Unity Odd Fellows further revised the rituals at the beginning of 1817. The political instability during this era and other social factors developed to further schisms that led to the creation of more than thirty-four (34) different affiliated Orders of Odd Fellows by the end of the 19th century.[2] Just to name a few:

- Grand United Order of Odd Fellows
- Independent Order of Odd Fellows, Manchester Unity

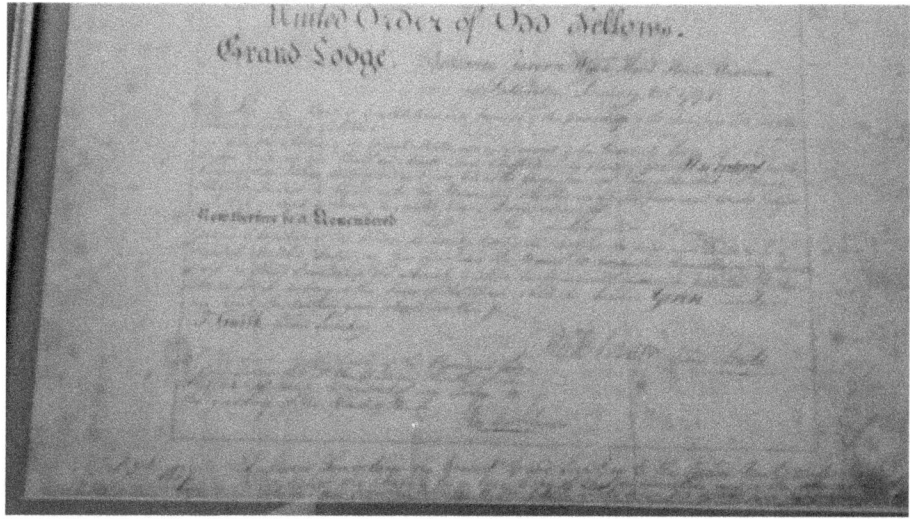

A Bond of Union to establish the Grand Lodge of the United Order of Odd Fellows on January 6, 1798 resulted to the dissolution of the Order of Patriotic Odd Fellows.

At the time of the merger, there were about fifty (50) Lodges affiliated with the Grand United Order of Odd Fellows. Thirty-nine (39) of which were located in London.

58 | Ancient Rites of Odd Fellowship

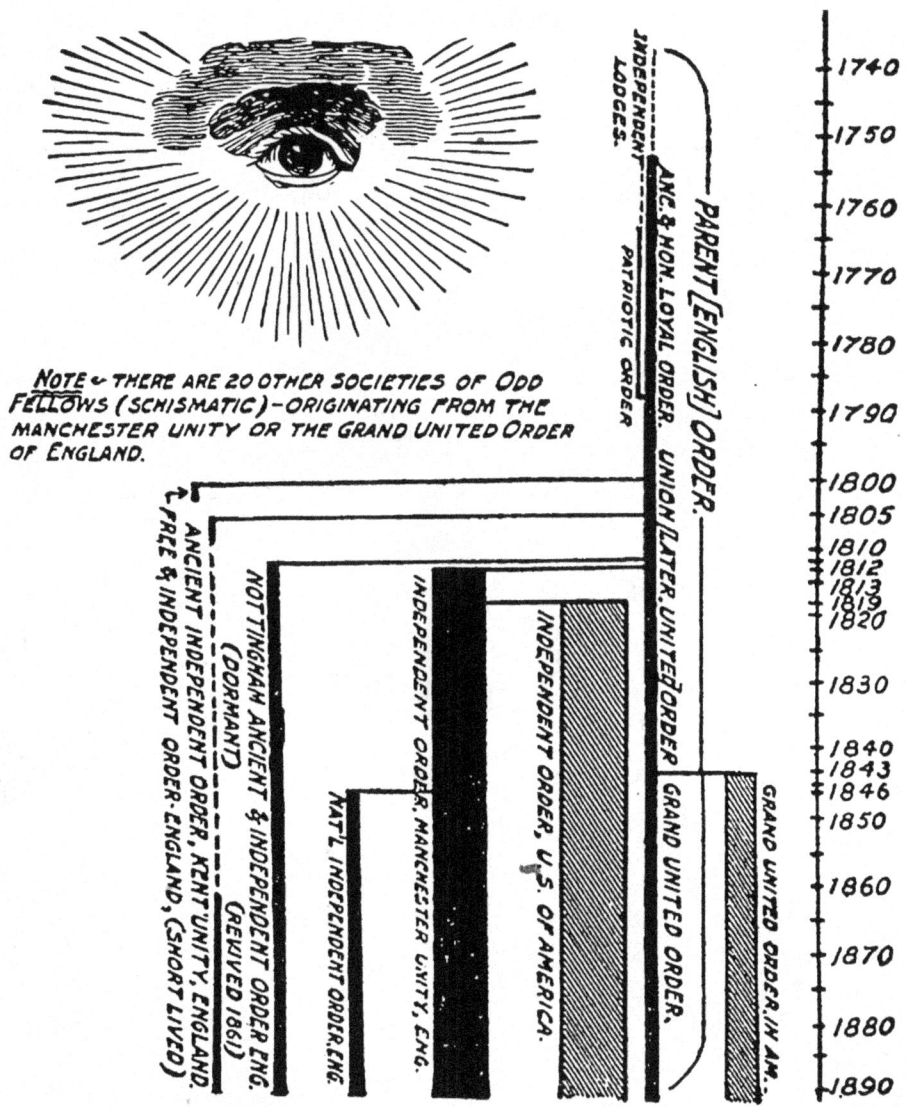

Chart showing the larger and more prominent English and American Orders of Odd Fellows, ancestry of each and date of origin.

Merger and Succession | 59

- Nottingham Ancient Imperial Order of Odd Fellows
- Ancient Noble Order of Odd Fellows, Bolton Unity
- British United Order of Odd Fellows
- Improved Independent Order of Odd Fellows, London Unity
- Albion Order of Odd Fellows
- Independent Order of Odd Fellows, Kingston Unity
- National Independent Order of Odd Fellows
- Ancient Independent Order of Odd Fellows, Kent Unity
- Independent Order of Odd Fellows, Wolverhampton Unity

All these affiliated Orders revised the ancient rituals and created their own version although some of the general principles, practices and symbols found in the 1797 rituals remained today or adopted in the higher degrees of the Encampment.

- End -

About the Author

Louie Blake Saile Sarmiento finished his Associate in Health Science Education in 2007; Bachelor of Science in Psychology with Certificate in Human Resource Management and Certificate in Women's Studies in 2010; Master of Arts in Industrial/Organizational Psychology in 2013; and Juris Doctor (law) degree in 2020. With a wide range of academic backgrounds, he uses various quantitative and qualitative research methodologies in his writings. He does not rely solely on old history books and manuals written many years ago but also conducts interviews, surveys, SWOT analysis, case studies and consults the most recent dissertations, thesis and expert opinions of historians, sociologists, psychologists, lawyers and other academic scholars.

He is instrumental in re-establishing Odd Fellowship in the Philippines. He is a Past Grand and Past District Deputy Sovereign Grand Master of the Independent Order of Odd Fellows. He is credited for connecting thousands of members from various countries when he created and managed the first social media groups and pages of the Independent Order of Odd Fellows from 2009-2019. He is also credited for writing and creating most of the modern literature and infographics about Odd Fellowship on the internet at a time when the organization had almost zero presence online, including the first YouTube videos and the Wikipedia entries about the Odd Fellows. Because of his contributions, he was appointed as Public Relations Coordinator and member of both the Communications Committee and the Revitalization Committee of the Sovereign Grand Lodge from 2012-2015. He was based at the Odd Fellows International Headquarters in North Carolina for an aggregate period of three years where he had full access and was able to read from cover-to-cover all available journals, history books, manuals, rituals and secret works of the Odd Fellows. He traveled widely for more than six years to conduct research and case studies about Odd Fellowship and similar fraternal organizations; visited hundreds of Lodges and several Grand Lodges across the United States and Canada; read and reviewed volumes of records, books and artifacts; observed meetings and initiations; and interviewed local, national and international leaders.

He is an advocate for the preservation of historical fraternal organizations, service clubs and civic associations. He is a member of all branches of the Independent Order of Odd Fellows (IOOF), including the Rebekah Lodge, Encampment and Patriarchs Militant. He is also affiliated with the Grand United Order of Odd Fellows (GUOOF); Ancient Mystic Order of Samaritans (AMOS); Noble Order of Muscovites (Muscovites); International Order of DeMolay (IOD); International Order of Free Gardeners (IOFG); Universal Druid Order (UDO); Ordo Supremus Militaris Templi Hierosolymitani - Regency (OSMTH); Knights of Rizal (KOR); The Fraternal Order of Eagles - Philippine Eagles (TFOE-PE); and Tau Gamma Phi or Triskelion Grand Fraternity (TGP). He now enjoys living a secluded and peaceful life while focusing on his career. As a hobby, he writes and collects books, antiques and artifacts related to fraternal organizations, service clubs and other civic associations.

Other Books by the Author

Title: Odd Fellows - Rediscovering More Than 200 Years of History, Traditions and Community Service

Publication date: April 26, 2019 (Last updated December 4, 2020)

Title: Odd Fellows: Brief History and Introduction to the Degrees, Symbols, Teachings, and Organization of Patriarchal Odd Fellowship

Publication date: October 26, 2020

Title: Odd Fellows Manual: Modern Guide to the Origin, History, Rituals, Symbols and Organization of the Independent Order of Odd Fellows

Publication date: December 3, 2020

Notes

I. Origin and History

1. Gist, *Culture Patterning in Secret Society Ceremonials*, University of North Carolina Press, North Carolina, 497-505.
2. Clawson, C*onstructing brotherhood: Class, Gender, and Fraternalism*, 15. "The lodges of the nineteenth and twentieth century America were the descendants of an earlier European fraternalism. Guilds, journeyman societies, religious confraternities, and village youth brotherhoods were all forms of fraternal association, making it one of the most widespread and culturally central modes of organization in the late medieval and early modern Europe."
3. The cultural origins of friendly societies like the Odd Fellows have been located in the demise of early modern craft guilds, see Cordery, *British friendly Societies, 1750-1914*, 17. See also Melling, *Discovering London's Guilds and Liveries*, 11. See also Moffrey, *A century of Odd Fellowship*, 6-17. See also the *Oddfellows Magazine*, September 1888. While the Masonic Order maintained intact the traditions of the Masons' craft guild, the Odd Fellows comprised a collection from all the others, which were not strong enough to form themselves to carry on a distinctive club.
4. By 1423 there were over 100 guilds. New ones formed, and amalgamations occurred. See Porter, London: *A social history*, 29. See also Melling, *Discovering London's Guilds and Liveries*, 34-106.
5. Smith, *English Gilds*, N. Trubner & Co., London. See also Dennis, *Discovering Friendly and Fraternal Societies*, 4.
6. See Curry, *The Red Blood of Odd Fellowship*, 62-65. See also Porter, *London: A social history*, 29.
7. Stillson, *The Official History of Odd Fellowship*, 33-37. See also Smith, *English Gilds*, N. Trubner & Co., London.
8. Porter, London: *A social history*, 29.
9. Ridley, *The Freemasons*, Chapter 3.
10. Reedy & Thurman, *A history of Denton Lodge, No.82, Independent Order of Odd Fellows*, 1859-2009, 7.
11. Melling, *Discovering London's Guilds and Liveries* (London: Shire Publications, 2003), 11; The cultural origins of friendly societies like the Odd Fellows have been located in the demise of early modern craft guilds, see Cordery, *British friendly Societies, 1750-1914*, 17.
12. Stillson, *The Official History of Odd Fellowship: The Three Link Fra-*

ternity, 21.

[13.] Allison Bryant, *Ecce Oriente*, 39.

[14.] See Grosh, *The Odd-Fellows Improved Pocket Manual*, 28-29. Grosh mentioned that the first members were toiling laborers. Their daily labor barely sufficed to procure them daily bread. When sickness came, aunt and terrible want was not far off. When one loses a job, he lacked the means to seek employment elsewhere and support their families meanwhile. When on the bed of disease or death, none could spare time to smooth the creased pillow, or moisten the fevered lips, or speak calmness to the delirious mind. See also Blainey, *Odd Fellows: A history of IOOF Australia*, 3, mentioned that the typical Odd Fellow in England in the eighteenth century was an artisan with an income higher than that of a laborer and lower than that of a clerk or self-employed tradesman.

[15.] Wallace, *The Odd-Fellows' Keepsake: A Concise History of Odd-Fellowship in the United States*, mentioned that the early English Lodges were supported, and their members relieved, by each member and visitor paying a penny to the secretary on entering the lodge. If a member needed aid, a sufficient sum will be given to him. If out of work, he was furnished with a card and funds to reach the next lodge.

[16.] Defoe, *Essay on Projects*, published in 1697.

[17.] Cordery, B*ritish Friendly Societies, 1750-1914*, Palgrave Macmillan, New York

[18.] Stillson, *The Official History of Odd Fellowship: The Three Link Fraternity*, 739.

[19.] Ibid.

[20.] Dennis, *Discovering Friendly and Fraternal Societies*, 13.

[21.] Aspinall, Douglas, & Smith, *English Historical Documents*, 319-322.

[22.] Ibid.

II. Merger and Succession

[1.] See Brooks, *The Official History and Manual of the Grand United Order of Odd Fellows*, 7-8.

[2.] Dennis, *Discovering Friendly and Fraternal Societies*, 92-94. See also entry for the Odd Fellows in Gilman, Peck and Colby, *The New International Encyclopedia*, 783. See also Weinbren, *The Oddfellows 1810-2010: 200 years of making friends and helping people*, 10.

References

Beharrell, Thomas. *Odd Fellows Monitor and Guide*. Indianapolis: Robert Douglass, 1883.

Beharrell, Thomas. *The Brotherhood: Being a Presentation of Odd Fellowship*. Indiana: Brotherhood Publishing Co., 1875.

Blainey, Goeffrey. *Odd Fellows: A History of IOOF Australia*. Australia: Allen & Unwin, 1991.

Brooks, Charles. *The Official History and Manual of the Grand United Order of Odd Fellows*. Pennsylvania: Odd Fellows Journal Print, 1903.

Bryant, Allison. *Ecce Oriente*. Michigan: CA Heritage. 2014.

Carnes, Mark. *Secret Ritual and Manhood in Victorian America*. New Haven: Yale University, 1989.

Clark, Peter. *British Clubs and Societies 1580-1800: The Origins of an Associational World*. New York: Oxford University Press, 2000.

Clark, Peter. *British Clubs and Societies: 1580-1800*. New York: Oxford University Press, 2002.

Clawson, Mary Ann. *Constructing Brotherhood: Class, Gender, and Fraternalism*. New Jersey: Princeton University Press, 1989.

Cordery, Simon. *British Friendly Societies, 1750-1914*. New York: Palgrave Macmillan, 2003.

Curry, Elvin James. *The Red Blood of Odd Fellowship*. Maryland: Elvin Curry, 1903.

Defoe, Daniel. An *Essay upon Projects*. London: R.R. for Tho. Cockerill, 1697.

Dennis, Victoria Solt. *Discovering Friendly and Fraternal Societies*. United Kingdom: Shire Publications, 2008.

Donaldson, Paschal. *The Odd Fellows Text Book*. Philadelphia: Moss & Brother, 1852.

Donaldson, Paschal. *The Odd Fellows' Pocket Companion*. Ohio: R.W. Carroll & Co, 1881.

Douglas, David Charles. *English Historical Documents*. United Kingdom: Oxford University Press, 1959.

Dumenil, Lynn. *The Oxford Encyclopedia of American Social History*. United States: Oxford University Press, 2012.

Epstein, Steven. *Wage labor and guilds in Medieval Europe*. North Carolina: University of North Carolina Press, 1991.

Gilman, Daniel Coit, Peck, Harry Thurston and Colby, Frank Moore. *The New International Encyclopedia*. New York: Dodd, Mead & Company, 1906.

Gist, Noel. *Patterning in Secret Society Ceremonials*. North Carolina: University of North Carolina Press, 1936.

Gosden, Peter Henry John Heather. *The Friendly Societies in England, 1815-1875*. United Kingdom: University of Manchester Press, 1961.

Greer, John Michael. *The Element Encyclopedia of Secret Societies*. New York: Barnes and Nobles, 2006.

Grosh, Aaron Burt. *The Odd Fellow's Manual*. Philadelphia: H.C. Peck & Theo Bliss, 1860.

Grosh, Aaron Burt. *A Manual of Odd Fellowship. New York:* New York: Clark & Maynard, 1882.

Melling, John Kennedy. *Discovering London's Guilds and Liveries*. United Kingdom: Shire Publications, 2002.

Moffrey, Robert. *The Rise and Progress of the Manchester Unity of the Independent Order of Oddfellows*. United Kingdom: Grand Master & Board of Directors of the Order, 1904.

Moffrey, Robert. *A Century of Odd Fellowship*. United Kingdom: Manchester Unity Independent Order of Oddfellows, 1910.

Parre, W.J. *Quatuor Coronatum: Being the Transactions of the Quatuor Coronati Lodge No. 2076, London, Volume 3* (London: W. J. Parre, 1840).

Porter, Roy. *London: A Social History*. United Kingdom: Penguin, 2000.

Powell, Benson. *The Triple Links*. Kansas: Ed G. Moore & Son, 1900.

Powley, Joseph. *Concise History of Odd Fellowship*. Toronto: The Grand Lodge of Ontario IOOF, 1943.

Powley, Joseph. *Concise History of Odd Fellowship (Revised edition)*. Toronto: Macoomb Publishing, 1952.

Reedy, Tom and Thurman, Nita. *Denton Lodge No.82, I.O.O.F.: A History 1859-2009*. Maine: Acme Bookbinding, 2009.

Rebold, Emmanuel, and Brennan, J. Fletcher. *A general History of Free-Masonry in Europe: Based upon the Ancient Documents Relating to and the Monuments Erected by this Fraternity from its foundation in the year 715 BC to present time*. Ohio: Cincinnati American Masonic publishing association, 1868.

Ridgely, James Lot. *History of American Odd Fellowship: The First Decade*. Baltimore: James Lot Ridgely, 1878.

Ridley, Jasper. *The Freemasons: A history of the world's most powerful secret society*. New York: Arcade Publishing, 2011.

Ross, Theodore. *Odd Fellowship: Its History and Manual*. New York: M.W. Hazen Co., 1888.

Smith, Joshua Toulmin. *English Gilds*. London: N. Trubner & Co., London, 1870.

Spry, James. *The History of Odd Fellowship: Its Origin, Tradition and Objectives*. London: J.R.H. Spry, 1866.

Streeter, Michael. *Behind Closed Doors*. United Kingdom: New Holland Publishers, 2008.

Stillson, Henry Leonard. *The Official History of Odd Fellowship*. Massachusetts: Fraternity Publishing Company, 1908.

Wallace, W.W. *The Odd-Fellows' Keepsake: A Concise History of Odd-Fellowship in the United States*. New York: Office of the Mirror of the Times, 1850.

Weinbren, Daniel. *The Oddfellows 1810-2010: 200 Years of Making Friends and Helping People*. Lancaster: Carnegie Publishing, 2012.

Ward-Stillson Co. *Ancient Ritual of the Order of Patriotic Odd Fellows: Revised and agreed to in the Grand Lodge held at London, England, March 12, 1797*. Michigan: Kalamazoo Publishing, n.d.

www.ingramcontent.com/pod-product-compliance
Lightning Source LLC
Chambersburg PA
CBHW070800050426
42452CB00012B/2416